Modern Middle East Nations
AND THEIR STRATEGIC PLACE IN THE WORLD

ALGERIA

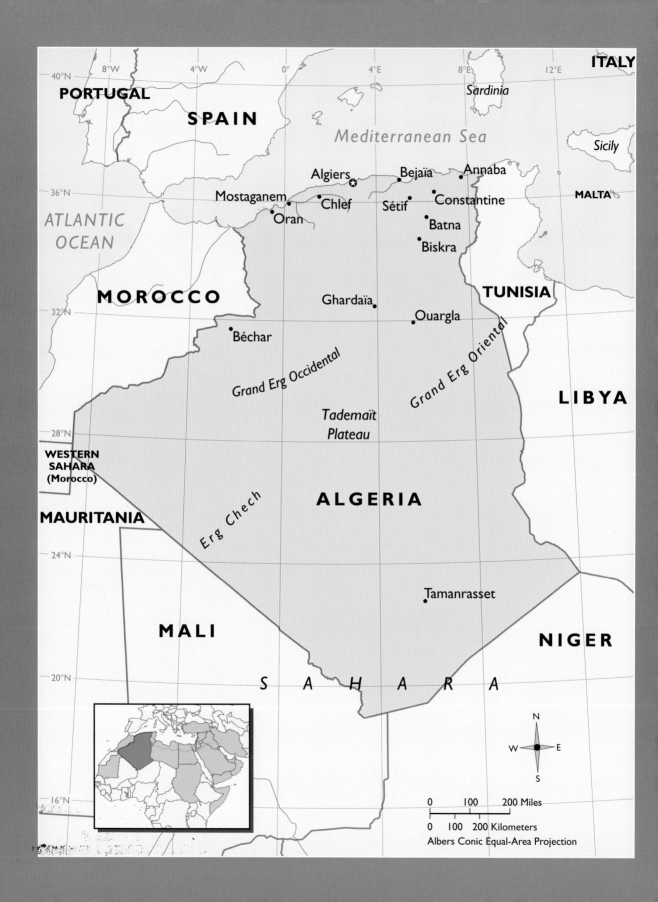

Modern Middle East Nations
AND THEIR STRATEGIC PLACE IN THE WORLD

ALGERIA

JAMES MORROW

MASON CREST PUBLISHERS
PHILADELPHIA

Produced by OTTN Publishing, Stockton, New Jersey

Mason Crest Publishers
370 Reed Road
Broomall, PA 19008
www.masoncrest.com

3 5 7 9 8 6 4 2

Library of Congress Cataloging-in-Publication Data

Morrow, James, 1974-
  Algeria / James Morrow.
    p. cm. — (Modern Middle East nations and their strategic
place in the world)
Summary: Discusses the geography, history, economy, government,
religion, people, foreign relations, and major cities of Algeria.
Includes bibliographical references and index.
  ISBN 1-59084-516-1
1. Algeria—Juvenile literature.   [1. Algeria.]   I. Title. II. Series.
DT275.M875 2003
965—dc21

                                    2002012998

Modern Middle East Nations
AND THEIR STRATEGIC PLACE IN THE WORLD

TABLE OF CONTENTS

Modern Middle East Nations
AND THEIR STRATEGIC PLACE IN THE WORLD

Dr. Harvey Sicherman, president and director of the Foreign Policy Research Institute, is the author of such books as *America the Vulnerable: Our Military Problems and How to Fix Them* (2002) and *Palestinian Autonomy, Self-Government and Peace* (1993).

Introduction

by Dr. Harvey Sicherman

Situated as it is between Africa, Europe, and the Far East, the Middle East has played a unique role in world history. Often described as the birthplace of religions (notably Judaism, Christianity, and Islam) and the cradle of civilizations (Egypt, Mesopotamia, Persia), this region and its peoples have given humanity some of its most precious possessions. At the same time, the Middle East has had more than its share of conflicts. The area is strewn with the ruins of fortifications and the cemeteries of combatants, not to speak of modern arsenals for war.

Today, more than ever, Americans are aware that events in the Middle East can affect our security and prosperity. The United States has a considerable military, political, and economic presence throughout much of the region. Developments there regularly find their way onto the front pages of our newspapers and the screens of our television sets.

7

Still, it is fair to say that most Middle Eastern countries remain a mystery, their cultures and religions barely known, their peoples and politics confusing and strange. The purpose of this book series is to change that, to educate the reader in the basic facts about the 23 states and many peoples that make up the region. (For our purpose, the Middle East also includes the North African states linked by ethnicity, language, and religion to the Arabs, as well as Somalia and Mauritania, which are African but share the Muslim religion and are members of the Arab League.) A notable feature of the series is the integration of geography, demography, and history; economics and politics; culture and religion. The careful student will learn much that he or she needs to know about ever so important lands.

A few general observations are in order as an introduction to the subject matter.

The first has to do with history and politics. The modern Middle East is full of ancient sites and peoples who trace their lineage and literature to antiquity. Many commentators also attribute the Middle East's political conflicts to grievances and rivalries from the distant past. While history is often invoked, the truth is that the modern Middle East political system dates only from the 1920s and was largely created by the British and the French, the victors of World War I. Such states as Algeria, Iraq, Israel, Jordan, Kuwait, Saudi Arabia, Syria, Turkey, and the United Arab Emirates did not exist before 1914—they became independent between 1920 and 1971. Others, such as Egypt and Iran, were dominated by outside powers until well after World War II. Before 1914, most of the region's states were either controlled by the Turkish-run Ottoman Empire or owed allegiance to the Ottoman sultan. (The sultan was also the caliph or highest religious authority in Islam, in the line of the prophet Muhammad's successors, according to the beliefs of the majority of Muslims known as the Sunni.) It was this imperial Muslim system that was ended by the largely British military victory over the Ottomans in World War I. Few of the leaders who emerged in the wake of this event were happy with the territories they were assigned or the borders, which were often drawn by Europeans. Yet, the system has endured despite many efforts to change it.

The second observation has to do with economics, demography, and natural resources. The Middle Eastern peoples live in a region of often dramatic geographical contrasts: vast parched deserts and high mountains, some with year-round snow; stone-hard volcanic rifts and lush semi-tropical valleys; extremely dry and extremely wet conditions, sometimes separated by only a few miles; large permanent rivers and *wadis*, riverbeds dry as a bone until winter rains send torrents of flood from the mountains to the sea. In ancient times, a very skilled agriculture made the Middle East the breadbasket of the Roman Empire, and its trade carried luxury fabrics, foods, and spices both East and West.

Most recently, however, the Middle East has become more known for a single commodity—oil, which is unevenly distributed and largely concentrated in the Persian Gulf and Arabian Peninsula (although large pockets are also to be found in Algeria, Libya, and other sites). There are also new, potentially lucrative offshore gas fields in the Eastern Mediterranean.

This uneven distribution of wealth has been compounded by demographics. Birth rates are very high, but the countries with the most oil are often lightly populated. Over the last decade, Middle East populations under the age of 20 have grown enormously. How will these young people be educated? Where will they work? The failure of most governments in the region to give their people skills and jobs (with notable exceptions such as Israel) has also contributed to large out-migrations. Many have gone to Europe; many others work in other Middle Eastern countries, supporting their families from afar.

Another unsettling situation is the heavy pressure both people and industry have put on vital resources. Chronic water shortages plague the region. Air quality, public sanitation, and health services in the big cities are also seriously overburdened. There are solutions to these problems, but they require a cooperative approach that is sorely lacking.

A third important observation is the role of religion in the Middle East. Americans, who take separation of church and state for granted, should know that most countries in the region either proclaim their countries to be Muslim or allow a very large role for that religion in public life. Among those with predominantly Muslim populations, Turkey alone describes itself as secular and prohibits avowedly religious parties in the political system. Lebanon was a Christian-dominated state, and Israel continues to be a Jewish state. While both strongly emphasize secular politics, religion plays an enormous role in culture, daily life, and legislation. It is also important to recall that Islamic law (*Sharia*) permits people to practice Judaism and Christianity in Muslim states but only as *Dhimmi*, protected but very second-class citizens.

Fourth, the American student of the modern Middle East will be impressed by the varieties of one-man, centralized rule, very unlike the workings of Western democracies. There are monarchies, some with traditional methods of consultation for tribal elders and even ordinary citizens, in Saudi Arabia and many Gulf States; kings with limited but still important parliaments (such as in Jordan and

Morocco); and military and civilian dictatorships, some (such as Syria) even operating on the hereditary principle (Hafez al Assad's son Bashar succeeded him). Turkey is a practicing democracy, although a special role is given to the military that limits what any government can do. Israel operates the freest democracy, albeit constricted by emergency regulations (such as military censorship) due to the Arab-Israeli conflict.

In conclusion, the MODERN MIDDLE EAST NATIONS series will engage imagination and interest simply because it covers an area of such great importance to the United States. Americans may be relative latecomers to the affairs of this region, but our involvement there will endure. We at the Foreign Policy Research Institute hope that these books will kindle a lifelong interest in the fascinating and significant Middle East.

A Berber man leads a camel through the Sahara Desert in the Ahaggar region. Unrest in Algeria over the past decade has threatened to split the country in two. Algerians are undecided about how much influence Islam should have on their government; another problem is the historic tension between the country's Arab and Berber populations.

Place in the World

Take a look at a map of Africa, and let your eye wander to the upper-left-hand corner of the continent. Up there, in between the crooked finger that is Morocco and the thumb-like nation of Tunisia, sits Algeria, a country almost three-and-a-half times the size of Texas. What would you expect to find there? Well, desert, for one thing; after all, most of the country is located in the western half of the world's largest desert, the Sahara. But Algeria is more than just a desert; in fact, in the northern part of the country a Mediterranean climate and rolling hills predominate, allowing for some of the best agriculture in North Africa.

It's not just geography and physical appearance that make Algeria a country divided. Even though the population is mostly Arab and 99 percent Muslim, the country is politically divided in many ways—ways that make it important to both the United States and the Arab world. And these divisions, which are the product of thousands of years of history, make Algeria's past a fascinating subject as well.

As part of North Africa, Algeria was one of the many regions to fall to the Arabs as they swept through the region spreading Islam more than a thousand years ago. But despite the Arabs' conquest, not all the country's citizens are ethnically Arab. Many **Berbers**—descendants of the original tribesmen who wandered the land thousands of years ago—can still be found in Algeria.

With nearly all of the people of Algeria following Islam, the influence of that religion on the government is strong, though not absolute. In Western countries like the United States, people take for granted the separation of religion from the government. However,

Thousands of Algerians have died during the violent civil war, which has been fought since 1992 for control of the country's political direction.

because Islamic law (**Sharia**) governs all aspects of daily life, it has a great influence over the governments of Muslim countries. The question of whether Algeria should be a fundamentalist Islamic state or a secular country has led to a bloody civil war in which more than 100,000 Algerians have been killed.

Historically, the Algerian government has been friendly to Western countries like the United States. In 1980, for example, Algerian diplomats worked to help secure the release of American citizens being held hostage at the U.S. Embassy in Tehran, Iran. More recently, Algeria condemned the September 11, 2001, terrorist attacks against the United States, and voiced support for the U.S.-led war on terrorism.

Algeria is important not just for its politics and religion—though books could be written on those subjects alone—but for what the country produces. Algeria's chief export and natural resource is petroleum—in fact, oil, natural gas, and related products make up 97 percent of everything the country sells overseas. And because Western nations like Italy, France, and the United States buy most of these products from Algeria, these countries have an economic stake in Algeria's future.

At the crossroads of European, Arab, and African civilizations, Algeria is one of those special places with a history, geography, culture, and people that make for compelling study. Algeria's history dates back more than 6,000 years. It has been part of many great empires of the past—Carthaginian, Roman, Umayyad, and Ottoman, to name a few—and more recently it was under French control. But while the history of Algeria is fascinating, the country's future remains in doubt. The civil war, and the terrorism that it has spawned, could indicate the destiny for much of the rest of the Arab world. Will other Arab countries follow Algeria's lead and fall into civil war, or will Algeria manage to find peace, showing the way for other Muslim nations in the Middle East?

The Sahara Desert stretches across much of North Africa, including southern Algeria. The Sahara is the world's largest desert; it covers between 800 to 1,200 miles (1,287 to 1,931 km) north to south, and at least 3,000 miles (4,828 km) east to west. Sandy stretches like this can be found in the Grand Erg Oriental region of eastern Algeria.

The Land

On most maps of the world, Algeria looks like little more than a vast empty space in North Africa. And this is at least partially true—once one gets away from the strip of fertile, habitable land along the coastline, Algeria is mostly empty space. And what a lot of space: Algeria is the second-largest country in Africa, after Sudan. But the popular conception of the country as nothing but a massive desert is a half-truth at best.

Algeria consists of three separate and distinct geographical regions: a coastal plain in the north that is home to most of the country's population, agriculture, and industry; a mountainous region known as the Tell (*tell* is the Arabic word for "hill"); and the vast sandy stretches of desert that have beguiled travelers, explorers, and writers for centuries.

As recently as the past century, Algeria supported large areas of forest, as much as 9.9 million acres (4 million hectares). Unfortunately, poor land management and environmental policies during the country's colonial period in the 19th century, combined with a series of forest fires, put an end to most of the country's timber. Reforestation programs begun by the government in the 1970s have begun to reverse some of this devastation, however.

THE COASTAL PLAIN AND THE TELL

Algeria has a relatively long coastline, stretching for 620 miles (998 kilometers) along the Mediterranean Sea. Although the country's weather can be irregular from year to year—meaning that pleasant weather in one year might lead to an extremely hot or relatively cold spell in the next one—this coast gives Algeria's northern region a pleasant, farmable climate. Not surprisingly, 90 percent of the country's population lives in this region, even though it comprises only about 15 percent of the country's total area. Many visitors to Algeria have even gone so far as to compare the climate of this region to that of southern California. In both areas average temperatures range from about 50° Fahrenheit (10° Celsius) in winter to 80°F (27°C) in summer. The fact that this region of Algeria lies along similar lines of latitude as southern California, and that Algeria borders a large body of water, makes the comparison even more obvious.

But it would be incorrect to push this comparison with southern California too far, considering the respective differences in

Opposite: Algeria, the second-largest country in Africa, can be divided into several east-west topographic zones. The strip of fertile land along the coast is separated from the Sahara by the Atlas Mountains. In the center of the country is the semiarid Tademaït Plateau, which has an average elevation of more than 3,600 feet (1,100 meters). To the south is the Sahara Desert and the Ahaggar Mountains, which include Algeria's highest peak.

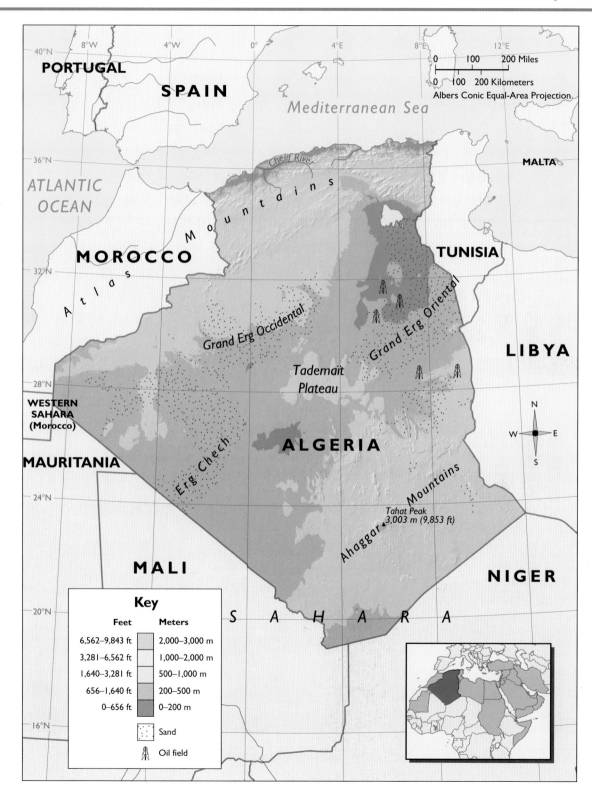

Key

Feet | Meters

6,562–9,843 ft — 2,000–3,000 m

3,281–6,562 ft — 1,000–2,000 m

1,640–3,281 ft — 500–1,000 m

656–1,640 ft — 200–500 m

0–656 ft — 0–200 m

Sand

Oil field

geography. The Tell Mountains repeatedly intrude into Algeria's coastal plain and keep it from being a continuous stretch of flat land suitable for settlement or growing crops.

This area's gently sloping hills have provided Algeria's inhabitants and occupiers with fertile soil for centuries; during their occupation, the French even managed to maintain vineyards that resulted in quality wines in some of these areas. But the encroaching mountains, though visually dramatic, create problems for farmers. In some valleys and basins, agriculture is virtually impossible due to dryness and extremes of summer heat that bake the earth and just about anything humans try to make grow in it.

This largely fertile area of Algeria comes to a dead halt in the

A cultivated field at the Touat Oasis. The irrigation channels used to transport water around an Algerian oasis are known as *fouggaras*.

northeast part of the country, near the Soummam River. As one moves east, the farms producing olives, figs, grapes, tobacco, fruits, vegetables, and cork give way to the massive mountain ranges of northeast Algeria. Further to the south, a series of salt lakes known as *sebkhas* or *chotts*, which stretch beyond Algeria into neighboring Tunisia and Morocco, break up the landscape. Since salt in the soil makes farming impossible, there is no agriculture in this region.

THE HIGH PLATEAU AND THE SAHARAN ATLAS

Beyond the relatively temperate regions of the Tell and the fertile coastal plain is where Algeria's geography gets interesting. The Tademaït Plateau—or as the French-speaking call it, the *Hautes Plateaux,* or high plateau—is a series of high steppe-like plateaus between 3,600 and 4,265 feet (1,100 and 1,300 meters) high in the west and around 1,312 feet (400 meters) high in the east. They mark the beginnings of what most people's conception of what a "desert" nation like Algeria should look like. In this region, one will find largely barren plains, where rainfall is scarce and the population is scattered. However, there are exceptions. Perhaps the best examples are the imperial post of Tlemcen, which was an important settlement from the 12th to 16th centuries, and the city of Constantine, which is the oldest continuously inhabited community in all of Algeria. In this city, picturesquely described by writer Alexandre Dumas as "an eagle's nest perched on the summit of a crag," one will find such sights as the Djamma el-Kebir Mosque and the spectacular Ahmed Bey Palace, a relic of Ottoman times, as well as the dramatic cliffs and gorges that surround the city.

The northern part of the plateau region receives an average of about 16 inches (41 cm) of rain each year, while the southern region receives about half that amount (8 inches/20 cm). Average temperatures range from about 48°F (9°C) in January to 80°F (27°C) in July.

The Saharan Atlas range, stretching in an arc through western Algeria from the Moroccan border to a hundred or so miles south of Algiers, is formed by three main mountains: the Ksour, the Amour, and the Ouled Nail. Unlike the High Plateau, and despite a forbidding appearance, this region is actually quite hospitable in many places due to the rainfall it receives. The Saharan Atlas includes regions of mountainous plains suitable for grazing, and many waterways that, while they eventually disappear into the desert, also manage to feed the wells of a good number of **oases**.

THE SAHARA

This region is perhaps the most legendary, most famous, and most misunderstood part of all of Algeria—or all of northern Africa, for that matter. The word *Sahara* conjures up images of an endless stretch of sand dunes, baked by the sun and ravaged by sandstorms, and populated only by Bedouins and the occasional intrepid (or foolhardy) explorer. While this sort of landscape *can* be found in Algeria's Saharan region, the overall nature of the Sahara desert in Algeria and elsewhere is somewhat different. In fact, only about 15 percent of the entire Sahara is sand dunes, while more than 70 percent is either rocky plateaus or mountainous areas.

In Algeria, the Sahara includes mountain ranges with peaks as high as 9,500 feet (2,900 meters), plains as flat as those in the American Midwest, and oases that not only have supported nomadic tribes for centuries but are also said to produce some of the most flavorful dates in the world. But because of its sparse population (only a few hardy souls make their home in the desert year-round) and "otherworldly" feel, this region is thought of by most Algerians as constituting a separate place in their national identity. This perspective hasn't always existed: prehistoric paintings found in the Sahara that date back 6,000 years depict a life that was not as bleak as it is today. Because the climate was different centuries ago, this region was once as verdant as it is today in the African **savanna**, or grasslands, to the south. Today, to a resident of Algiers or another of the country's coastal cities the vast, hot, sandy desert feels about as far away in the mind, if not in actual distance, as the cold, snowy mountains of Alaska feel to an American student growing up in, say, Los Angeles, New York, or Miami.

Only about one-quarter of the Algerian Sahara, a region that stretches for 920 miles (1,500 km) from the Saharan Atlas south to

The Geography of Algeria

Location: Northern Africa, bordering the Mediterranean Sea, between Morocco and Tunisia

Area: almost 3.5 times the size of Texas
  total: 919,590 square miles (2,381,740 sq km)
  land: 919,590 square miles (2,381,740 sq km)
  water: 0 square miles (0 sq km)

Borders: Libya, 610 miles (982 km); Mali, 855 miles (1,376 km); Mauritania, 288 miles (463 km); Morocco, 969 miles (1,559 km); Niger, 594 miles (956 km); Tunisia, 600 miles (965 km); Western Sahara, 26 miles (42 km)

Coastline: 620 miles (998 km)

Climate: arid to semiarid; mild, wet winters with hot, dry summers along coast; drier with cold winters and hot summers on high plateau

Terrain: mostly high plateau and desert; some mountains; narrow, discontinuous coastal plain

Elevation extremes:
  lowest point: Chott Melrhir, 131 feet (40 meters) below sea level
  highest point: Tahat, 9,853 feet (3,003 meters)

Natural hazards: mountainous areas subject to severe earthquakes; mudslides and floods in rainy season

Source: Adapted from CIA World Factbook, 2002.

A sandstone rock formation in the Ahaggar region of southern Algeria. More than 70 percent of the Sahara Desert in Algeria is gravel and rock, rather than broad stretches of sandy dunes.

the borders of Mali and Niger, is sandy desert in the traditional sense. In these areas, most prominently the Grand Erg Oriental (from the Arabic word *erg*, or *areg*, meaning "sand dunes") in the northern Sahara, vast dunes as high as 16 feet (5 meters) are evenly spaced for as far as the eye can see. It is this sort of region that is popularly thought of as "Saharan." The Grand Erg Oriental is the location of some of the country's most beautiful oases. Many traditional Berber tribes call this region home. As one moves south towards Mali, the rolling dunes vanish and give way to a blank, arid zone that is the home of nomads.

The rest of the Sahara is characterized by mountains, sandstone plateaus, and even dramatic gorges cut by ancient rivers. Today, there are still some rivers (most of which only flow seasonally) at the northern edge of the Sahara, but with the exception of oases, the majority of this region is as barren as one would expect. Among the most striking features of the region is the valley of the M'Zab, populated by a breakaway Islamic sect known as the Mozabites, who have settled in five villages along an oasis 6.2 miles (10 km) long. (This oasis supports, along with 100,000 human inhabitants, 270,000 palm trees.) Another striking feature is the Ahaggar Mountain range, whose peaks range from between 8,500 to 9,500 feet (2,600 and 3,000 meters). Here, high altitudes bring bitterly cold temperatures, and the only real precipitation is the occasional snowfall.

In 1975, the Algerian government began to plant a belt of trees just south of the Saharan Atlas Mountains. This was intended to keep the desert from drifting northward. The trees stretch along the foot of the mountains for about 930 miles (1,500 km).

Crowds in Algiers celebrate independence, June 5, 1962. The fight for Algerian independence from French control lasted eight years and cost hundreds of thousands of lives.

History

A lgeria—or rather, the plot of land that Algeria sits on—has a history that stretches back through at least 6,000 years of civilization. Historians have made this time estimation based on their findings of ancient cave paintings in the country's mountains that date back at least that far.

From the early days of Algerian prehistory to the 21st century, Algeria has been a witness to many of the great events in world history. (Throughout this chapter the word "Algeria" will refer to the physical area covered by the current country, not necessarily the modern nation itself.) And understanding Algeria's history—which includes the rise of Islam and the downfall of the Ottoman Empire, two chapters in history that still resonate throughout the Middle East today—provides a better understanding of the world today.

THE BERBERS, THE CARTHAGINIANS, AND THE ROMANS

The first humans probably took up residence in Algeria about 6,000 years ago. They were Berber tribesmen, a group whose descendants still live in the region today. The first significant encounters the Berbers had with the outside world took place around 3,000 years ago. During this time the Phoenicians, a seagoing and commercial people who lived in the eastern Mediterranean region, sailed away from their home cities in the area that is now Lebanon and began to establish trading posts along the North African coast. Eventually, these posts grew into Phoenician settlements. Around 800 B.C., the Phoenicians established a trading post at Carthage, in what is now Tunisia. Within a few centuries these Carthaginians, as we now call them, had established more trading posts of their own along the coastline. When the Phoenician city-states to the east were conquered by the Assyrians and Persians, the city of Carthage and the coastal territories it ruled in northern Africa, including Algeria, were left to govern themselves.

In the interior of Algeria, meanwhile, the Berbers had developed their own civilization, one based largely on agriculture and trade. For the most part, these inland farmers were able to maintain good relations with the seafaring Carthaginians. This wasn't always the case, however. On occasion Berbers were captured and sold into slavery by the Carthaginians, and at other times Berbers were forced to pay **tribute** to the rulers of Carthage. But for the most part the Berbers and the Carthaginians managed to get along well for several centuries. By the time Carthage became involved in a series of wars with Rome, another powerful city-state located across the Mediterranean in Italy, Berbers made up a large part of the Carthaginian army.

The wars between Carthage and Rome were called the Punic

These cave paintings, found in the Tassili des Ajjer Mountains in southern Algeria, were probably created by the earliest inhabitants of the region. They may have been made more than 6,000 years ago.

Wars. The word "Punic," which refers to the Carthaginians' civilization, comes from the Latin word *poeni*, which means "Phoenician."

The power of Carthage waned in the wake of the First Punic War (264–241 B.C.). When the war ended, the Carthaginians were not able to pay their **mercenary** soldiers, and the troops (mostly Gauls and members of other European tribes) rebelled. Their rebellion—called the Revolt of the Mercenaries—was successful, as the rebels captured several of Carthage's provinces in northern Africa. The Berbers became allies of Hamilcar Barcas, the Carthaginian leader, in the fight to defeat the rebels. When the rebellion was all over in

238 B.C., the Berbers wound up controlling much of the northern area around Carthage; the power of Carthage was in decline; and several Berber kingdoms were on the rise in the hinterland. These circumstances culminated in what some historians have called the high point of Berber civilization—the reign of King Masinissa in the second century B.C.

By this point, it was no longer the Carthaginians who were playing the dominant foreign role in Algeria, but rather the Roman Empire, which was at the same time expanding all across the ancient world. Carthage's hold over northern Africa had ended with the end of the Second Punic War (218–202 B.C.), and by 146 B.C. Rome had utterly destroyed Carthage itself. While the Berbers were able to hold the Romans off for about 100 years

The ancient Roman ruins at Djemila are among the best-preserved in North Africa. In the first century A.D. a Roman military garrison was stationed here (at the time the town was called Cuicul). The columns pictured here once held the roof over a market, while the table was used for measuring liquids or grains. The Romans abandoned this Algerian outpost in the fifth century.

after the death of the last member of Masinissa's family, in A.D. 24 the Romans took over the rest of the region.

The Roman Empire may have been the greatest political and military power of the ancient world, but that does not mean everyone was happy to see its soldiers marching on their shores. This was especially true for the Berbers, who lost control over their land, which was suddenly pressed into service as "the granary of the Empire." At the same time, increasing urbanization ordered by Rome led many Berbers to lose connection to their traditional ways. As happened across the Roman Empire, from one end of the Mediterranean to the other, the Romans built cities and towns according to uniform grid-like plans, the ruins of which can still be seen throughout Algeria and North Africa today.

But while the Romans were powerful, and the North African region remained important to them, they did not spend much effort, time, or money on keeping Algeria in line. It is estimated that the Romans kept a relatively small **garrison** of about 28,000 troops in Algeria, and a large number of these soldiers were local mercenaries rather than legionnaires imported from Rome. Interestingly, the Romans' stricter attempts at control in their other holdings wound up giving Algeria another one of its periodic infusions of people from the wider world: rebellious Jews from Roman Palestine were exiled to Algeria, giving the country a Jewish population that thrived and survived until the eve of the modern nation's independence from France. (Interestingly, several Berber tribes converted to Judaism as a result.) Algeria's first Christians arrived during the period of Roman rule as well.

Like all empires, Rome eventually fell. In A.D. 429 the Vandals, a Germanic tribe that had been ravaging the Roman Empire in Europe, crashed across the Strait of Gibraltar into Africa. This was the beginning of the end for Roman control of Algeria. Just a decade later, in 439, the Vandal king Gaiseric conquered the remaining Roman provinces in Africa. What followed was nearly 100 years of chaos in Algeria, as the Berbers reemerged to claim power, independent kingdoms established themselves and clashed with one another, and the cities and towns of which the Romans had been so proud were overrun by marauders.

This period lasted until 533, when the Byzantine Empire reasserted control over northern Africa. The Byzantine Empire, based out of Constantinople (the modern-day city of Istanbul, in Turkey), was the eastern half of the Roman Empire; it had broken away about 200 years earlier. During the fifth century, the Byzantines had survived the attacks that had destroyed Rome and the western empire. The Byzantine emperor Justinian, who ruled from 527 to 565, expanded the empire's territory by conquering lands in northern Africa, the eastern Mediterranean, and Italy. He established a political organization so the regions could be ruled from Constantinople. Under this system the Berbers wound up retaining and expanding control of much of their territory. (It is interesting to note that the modern-day adjective "Byzantine" comes from this empire; today this word is often used to describe a bureaucracy or organization that is characterized by red tape, leadership struggles, and power that flows through complicated and ultimately ineffective channels.)

THE COMING OF ISLAM

While the Byzantines were pursuing their long-distance administration of Algeria, thousands of miles away on the Arabian Peninsula events were playing out that would change the world. The rise of Islam and its further expansion is of critical importance to the past 1,400 years of Algerian history.

Sometime around A.D. 570—the exact date is uncertain—a man named Muhammad was born in the town of Mecca on the Arabian Peninsula, in the land now known as Saudi Arabia. At the time, the

This fortress, overlooking a North African town, dates from the Byzantine period. The Byzantine Empire took control of the Mediterranean coast of Africa in the sixth century, but were forced from the region by the start of the eighth century.

people of this land believed in a variety of pagan and **polytheistic** religions. Although he was orphaned as a boy, Muhammad wound up under the protection of his uncle who trained him to be a merchant and trader. At the age of 25 he married a wealthy widow named Khadija, and they started a family. And for 15 years or so Muhammad enjoyed a peaceful and prosperous life as a respected member of society. Then the visions started.

It is not known exactly when it happened, but when Muhammad was in his early forties, he began to feel spiritually restless, hear voices, and see visions. Muhammad soon began preaching that there was only one god, Allah, and told others of the messages he had received from him.

Muhammad began to attract a small band of followers, but they soon ran afoul of the local authorities, who were upset by the new brand of **monotheism** (or belief in one god) that he was preaching with increasing success. The authorities plotted to kill Muhammad.

When Muhammad learned of their plans in 622, he left Mecca and made his way to Medina, another city in the region. There a new religion, which would become known as Islam, was born. (The name comes from the Arabic word for "submission," specifically to the will of God.) And although Muhammad died just ten years later after dictating the **Qur'an** (also spelled Koran), the Islamic holy book, the seeds of Islam as an expansionist religion were planted as he charged his followers to spread the faith to non-believers.

After the death of Muhammad, Islam split into several sects. The two major divisions in Islam, between the Sunni and Shiite Muslims, arose from a dispute over who would succeed Muhammad as caliph ("deputy of the prophet," or the leader of the Muslims) after his death. Muhammad's only heir was his daughter, Fatimah, but she was not eligible to succeed him because she was a woman. Most followers supported the decision of an assembly of Muhammad's advisors, which selected a man named Abu Bakr as the first caliph. Although Abu Bakr was a close friend of Muhammad (and the father of the prophet's second wife), he was not related by blood. The assembly chose the Islamic leader on the strength of his faith, not because he was descended from Muhammad.

A smaller group of followers (Shiites) disagreed. They believed the caliph should be chosen from Muhammad's descendants or relatives, and supported Fatimah's husband, Ali, who was also Muhammad's cousin, as his rightful successor. Ali was selected as the fourth caliph, but when he was killed in 661 his son Hussein was passed over for the position. In response the Shiites broke away from the Sunni Muslims.

Under the leadership of the caliphs, the Arab Muslims made war on their neighbors until they had forcibly converted not just the people living on the Arabian Peninsula but empires like Persia (now Iran) to the faith.

This page from a 12th-century Arabic manuscript shows a caravan passing a fortified town. Although the Arabs had conquered most of North Africa by the eighth century, spreading their religion among the people, it would take some 400 years before the Berbers were "Arabized."

It wasn't long before Islam was ready to break out of the Arabian Peninsula. Algeria and North Africa were in the crosshairs of the expansion. By 641, Islam had made its way into Egypt, and as a result of Arab military expeditions that took place from 642 to 669, the religion spread into Africa.

Members of a Muslim ruling dynasty, the Umayyads, wanted to dominate the Mediterranean region. They began to establish bases on the coast of northern Africa. Around 680, an Arab commander named Abu al Muhajir led his army into Algeria; he persuaded the ruler of a powerful confederation of Christian Berbers to become a Muslim and accept the rule of the Umayyads. By 711 Umayyad forces, assisted by Berber converts to Islam, had conquered all of North Africa.

However, although most of the Berbers accepted Islam they did not necessary support the Arab-dominated caliphate. In part this was because the Arabs treated the Berbers as second-class citizens. The Berbers were forced to pay heavy taxes, and in some cases were enslaved by the Arabs. Discontent turned into open revolt in 739–40 when many Berbers joined with members of an Islamic sect called the Kharijites. The Kharijites were extreme fundamentalists who had split from the caliphate (the Arabic word *khariji* means "those who leave") nearly 85 years earlier. Since then, they had been fighting the rule of the Umayyads in the Middle East. Many Berbers were attracted to the sect because of its promise of equality for all people.

After the revolt, Kharijites established a number of small kingdoms in North Africa. These did not last long, and by 800 the caliphate had retaken control of much of Algeria. However, some parts of the region remained under the influence of **Ibadi Islam**, which had developed from Kharijite beliefs. The court of the Rustumids, a series of elected **imams** who ruled much of the central **Maghreb** from 761 to 909, was known for justice and as a center of Muslim learning in such fields as astronomy, theology, mathematics, law, and astrology.

THE FATIMIDS AND THE ZIRIDS

Near the end of the ninth century, missionaries who represented a subgroup of Shia Islam called Ismaili converted a group of Berbers, the Kutama, who were living in what today is Algeria. Once converted to Ismaili, these Berbers attacked major cities in Tunisia, capturing Al Qayrawan in 909. The Ismaili imam, Ubaydallah, declared himself caliph and established Mahdia, in Tunisia, as his capital. This was the start of the Fatimid dynasty, named after Fatimah, the daughter of Muhammad, from whom Ubaydallah claimed descent.

The Fatimids continued to spread their rule. In 911, they invaded Morocco, destroying the powerful imamates at Tahirt and Sijilmasa. Ibadi Muslims from Tahirt fled south over the Atlas Mountains; they later moved to Oued Mzab in Algeria, where Ibadi has remained the dominant form of Islam.

By 969 the Fatimids had conquered Egypt, and in 972 the Fatimid ruler Al Muizz made Cairo the country's capital. With their focus on Egypt and the Middle East, the Fatimids left control of the Algeria region to the Zirids, a Berber dynasty that had founded the towns of Miliana, Médéa, and Algiers. The Zirids ruled from 972 to 1148. During this time Bejaïa, a port in northern Algeria, became the most important seaport in the Maghreb.

Despite the power of the Fatimids, this period was often marked by conflict and political instability. Tribes of Berbers often fought each other, as well as raiders from Europe, Muslim Almoravids, and Arab Bedouins. The arrival in the 11th century of large numbers of Bedouin (sent by the Fatimid rulers to weaken the power of the Zirids) forced many Berbers to move to the interior of the country. Most of those Berbers who remained became "Arabized"—they accepted the Arabic language and began to follow Arab customs.

The process of Arabizing the Berbers had taken nearly four centuries—significant, considering how quickly the Berbers had accepted Islam. There are several reasons this process took so long. The Berbers resisted Arabization because they wanted to preserve and protect their language and culture. In some cases, that resistance took the form of unorthodox Islamic beliefs, such as Shia or Ibadi Islam. Another persistent form of Islam was Sufi, a hybrid religion that combines elements of Islam with mysticism and, in Algeria, incorporated the traditional beliefs and saints of Berber religious cults.

THE COMING OF THE OTTOMAN EMPIRE

From the 11th through the 16th centuries, Muslims and Christians fought in Europe and the Middle East. Between 1095 and 1291, Christian European armies made a series of invasions of the Middle East called the **Crusades** to recapture holy sites from the Muslims. Spain, which had been conquered by Muslims from North Africa during the 8th century, was also a battleground for more than six centuries. The Spanish finally forced the Muslims out in 1492.

In the east, a new power was rising in present-day Turkey. In 1453, the Ottoman Turks finally conquered Constantinople, renaming it Istanbul and ending the power of the once-glorious Byzantine Empire. In its place rose a new empire—the Ottoman Empire. During the rule of Sultan Selim I (1512–20) the empire expanded, and it reached its height under the rule of his son Suleyman (1520–66), controlling a vast area of Asia, eastern Europe, and northern Africa.

The Ottoman Empire became known for its efficient bureaucracy and administration. The Ottomans indirectly ruled cities in Algeria and in other parts of the empire. The sultan was considered to be the political and religious leader of the empire, and all decisions were believed to come from him. In reality, the government was run by a series of bureaucratic levels. The sultan and his advisers were constrained by strict rules. At the farther reaches of the empire, local potentates controlled various districts. Although they operated in the name of the sultan, the potentates were not directly controlled by him in any meaningful way. If the local rulers did not stay in line, however, the Ottomans had a strong army that could be used to maintain the peace. A key element of this was an elite corps of well-armed, well-trained soldiers known as **_Janissaries_**.

The Ottomans used pirates to help bring the Algeria region under its control; two bold Greek brothers, Aruj and Khayr ad-Din, were particularly effective. The younger brother had a red beard, leading Europeans to nickname him Barbarossa, or "Red Beard." In 1518, the brothers, aided by Janissaries, took control of the Algerian coast. After Aruj died Khayr ad-Din remained in power. From his base in Algiers, much of the rest of the region, extending into Tunisia, was brought under Ottoman control. The Ottoman sultan was so pleased that in 1533 he brought Barbarossa to Istanbul and placed him in charge of the Ottoman fleet. In 1544 Khayr ad-Din's son Hasan was made the governor of the region.

But because of the distance from the Ottoman capital, restiveness within Algeria, and the difficulties the Ottomans had coping with their own growing bureaucracy, Algeria was not to remain firmly under the sultan's thumb for long. In 1587, a new system was put in place whereby governors served for three-year terms; these rulers, known as pashas, were the Ottomans' representatives in Algeria. Turkish became the official language and locals were excluded from government positions.

This system would prove to be the downfall of the Ottoman regime in Algeria. Because the Janissaries relied on the pashas for their salaries, and because the pashas were regularly delinquent

An Italian artist from Florence painted this picture of Khayr ad-Din (1483–1546) in 1550, four years after the pirate leader's death. Barbarossa founded the kingdom of Algiers, and perfected the practice of raiding the ships of Europeans in the Mediterranean. Pirate raids from the so-called Barbary Coast, which was named for Barbarossa, continued until the early 19th century.

in paying the troops, a series of rebellions occurred in the 1600s, culminating in the head of the Janissaries seizing power in 1659. But in 1671 power shifted back, as a representative of the Sultan overthrew the new leadership and took the title of **dey**. This leader was in essence a dictator constrained by some constitutional limits, and by 1710 the dey, with his council of leaders, had managed to retake a measure of control from the palace in Istanbul. As a result Algeria, although officially still part of the Ottoman Empire, was for a while effectively independent.

Although the dey had great power, there were rules that restricted his authority. Once elected, the dey legally could not be removed; however, 14 of 29 deys were assassinated between 1671 and 1830. Despite occasional violence, though, this period in Algerian history was relatively orderly.

A "CIVILIZING MISSION"

The piracy originating on the coast of northern Africa—a region that would become known to Westerners as the **Barbary Coast**, after Barbarossa—did not decrease after the Ottomans took over. In fact, by the late 18th century the Barbary pirates were becoming more of a problem for Western nations—including the newly independent United States, which in an early naval action sent warships to Algiers to rescue Americans being held captive there by pirates.

But it was France that had the most problems with Algeria. In addition to provocation from the Barbary pirates, France had domestic problems. It hoped to end both by colonizing Algeria.

In 1827, the French monarch Charles X launched a naval blockade against Algiers after one of his diplomats was on the receiving end of a perceived (and probably nonexistent) insult from a local official. The idea was that by giving the French people a common cause to rally around—namely, an insult to French honor—the king would be able to distract attention from the country's otherwise abominable military, economic, and political situation. But the blockade didn't achieve the king's desired goals. Taking the next step, the French, using plans originally drawn up by Napoleon himself, blasted their way onto Algerian shores on June 12, 1830, as part of what they diplomatically termed a "civilizing mission."

The pillage of Algiers must go down as one of the low moments of European colonialism. After fighting the dey's army for three weeks, 34,000 French soldiers made their way into the city of Algiers, destroying homes and buildings, desecrating mosques and cemeteries, and even helping themselves to the money in the vaults of the Algerian treasury.

The attack on Algeria could not distract the people of France from their problems at home forever, and soon after Algiers was captured the French rose up and forced Charles X from the throne. However, though the leaders of the new government in France were opposed to the invasion of Algeria, they found themselves unable to pull out—and so, for reasons of "national prestige," the occupation continued. In 1834, France decided to **annex** all the land in Algeria it had occupied to that point. By 1847, the western parts of the country fell to French control, and in 1871 the Kabylie Mountain region suffered the same fate, establishing the borders of what we know today as Algeria.

Meanwhile, France's "civilizing mission" had begun in earnest. The government sought to impose French values, language, and culture on the centuries-old Muslim society in Algeria. The words

Charles X (1757–1830) became king of France in 1824. Three years later the king ordered a blockade of Algeria, and eventually French troops invaded the country. Although the king would ultimately be forced from the throne in 1830, Algeria would remain a French colony for more than 130 years.

of the French writer Alexandre Dumas, who had been sent to Algeria by the French government to write a series of dispatches introducing France's people to their new colony, was typical of this superior attitude. "Algiers, headquarters of the dreaded Barbary pirates ever since the Middle Ages, the traditional stronghold of the Deys who defied Europe for centuries, suffered considerable damage during the bombardment that preceded the victory of our forces in 1830," wrote Dumas, happily describing the city under French rule. "Except for the Grand Mosque, which survived, all the lower part of the town behind the harbor was demolished, and has now been rebuilt in the French manner."

It wasn't just architecture and other treasures that were destroyed in France's quest to create a colony in its own image on the other side of the Mediterranean. Within the first two decades of their occupation, the French also destroyed whatever there was of a local Arab middle class, and kept the rest of the population docile under the leadership of French-appointed holy men who were known derisively as the *beni oui oui*—loosely translated, the "Tribe of the Yes Men."

Yet as much as France wanted to strip Algeria of its Arab identity, no attempt was made to make the local population into full-fledged French citizens. Even when Muslim Algerians did receive an education in the French manner, they were looked down upon by the French. Adding insult to injury, these educated Algerians were mistrusted by their own countrymen for trying to imitate the habits and manners of the French occupiers.

To illustrate just how strongly the French in Algeria felt about this rising class of French-educated Algerians, one need only look at their reaction to a 1936 plan to grant French citizenship to a select group of 20,000 Algerians. To protest the idea, every French mayor in every Algerian town resigned.

By the start of the 20th century, there were more than a million

The French artist Alfred Henri Darjou painted this scene of Emperor Napoleon III visiting Algeria in May 1865. Napoleon III placed Algeria under the control of a military government, and issued a decree recognizing the differences in cultural background between the Muslims and French settlers (called *colons*) in Algeria. He attempted to keep the two populations separate. Napoleon also offered full citizenship to any Arab Algerian; however, this required acceptance of French courts, rather than *Sharia*, as the basis of civil law. This effectively meant that the Muslim Arabs would have to give up their religious beliefs to become citizens, and very few Algerians were willing to do this.

French settlers living in Algeria. These imported Frenchmen controlled most of the manufacturing, mining, agriculture, and trade in the country. The Arabs and Berbers of Algeria were unable to improve their situation through political activity. In fact, the approximately 4 million Muslim residents of Algeria had no representation in the country's general assembly, and by 1915 fewer than 50,000 Muslims were permitted to vote in local elections. At the same time, though, the native Algerians paid the greatest share of the taxes.

THE BIRTH OF NATIONALISM

After the end of the First World War, the seeds of Algerian nationalism took root. At first, few residents of Algeria, Arab or Berber, were involved in the nationalist movement. Most of the early supporters were Algerians who had served with the French forces during World War I or gone to France as laborers. There these Algerians saw the democratic freedoms available in France but not in Algeria. The rise of Arab nationalism in the Middle East in the 1920s and 1930s contributed to the Algerian movement.

The first attempts at fomenting Algerian nationalism came from communist parties inside both Algeria and France, which were in turn supported by the communist government of the Soviet Union. The communist-influenced Algerian organization Star of North Africa, led by charismatic Ahmed Messali Hadj, was the first to call for independence, in 1927. But a thirst for religious nationalism also played a part; in 1935, an Islamic group known as the *ulema*, or "religious teachers," began making demands for freedom similar to those of the communist nationalists. One of the most influential of these religious reformers was Abd al-Hamid Ben Badis.

The Arab Muslim nationalists, whether inspired by religious or communist ideals, demanded three things—independence from France, the end of French cultural oppression, and the adoption of Arabic as the official language of a new nation. It should be noted that Berbers also supported the nationalist movement and its rejection of French culture; however, they wanted Berber culture and language to be recognized as part of an independent Algeria also. This issue remains at the heart of Arab-Berber tensions in Algeria today.

Though the French settlers in Algeria, and many citizens in France, rejected these demands, those people agitating for Algerian independence were not without friends in the government in Paris. Many liberal French politicians supported at least some of the nationalists' goals during the 1930s.

With the outbreak of World War II, and France's quick capitulation to Germany in 1940, the Algerian independence movement came to a halt. The French surrender led to the establishment of a new government, known as the Vichy regime, which controlled unoccupied France (Germany occupied three-fifths of the country). This collaborationist government was never recognized as legitimate by Great Britain and other Allied powers; instead the Allies supported the Free French government led by Charles de Gaulle, which continued to resist the Germans. However, Vichy rule over France's colonies, such as Algeria, provided new problems for Muslims and Berbers in Algeria. The Vichy government carried out the anti-Semitic laws imposed by Nazi Germany, leaving members of Algeria's Jewish community vulnerable to deportation to concentration camps.

Vichy control in Algeria was overthrown after Allied troops landed at Algiers and Oran in November 1942. Free French leaders then asked Algerians to join the Allied effort to defeat Nazi Germany. In response, Algerian leaders like Ferhat Abbas demanded the right for Algerians to develop their own political, economic, and social programs. This would have given Algeria some autonomy, though the country would have remained a colony of France. When the French government rejected Abbas' proposals, he changed his position and began demanding Algeria's complete independence. He was soon joined by Messali Hadj and other Algerian nationalist leaders.

General Charles de Gaulle, circa 1940, the year France surrendered to Nazi Germany. When France fell, de Gaulle (1890–1970) led the Free French resistance, which fought with the British and Americans in North Africa during World War II. By 1943, the provisional French government was based in Algiers.

In 1958 de Gaulle again became the leader of France, in part because of unrest in Algeria. Although initially he promised that Algeria would remain a French colony forever, he soon changed his views and was willing to let Algeria become independent.

As the war came to a close, Algerian nationalists held demonstrations to call attention to their desire for liberation. Tensions exploded during a march on May 8, 1945—V-E Day, the day set aside to celebrate the Allied victory over Germany—when Franco-Algerian police clashed with nationalists in the city of Sétif. Rioting began throughout the country, and the French army stepped in to restore order. In the fighting that followed, 1,500 Algerian Muslims were killed, according to official French figures. (Other estimates put the figure at more than 6,000 killed.) Abbas, Hadj, and other leaders were arrested.

THE ALGERIAN INSURRECTION

After World War II ended, Algerian demands for independence increased. Activist groups—many with paramilitary leanings—were

French soldiers search a civilian on a street in Algiers, March 1962. The Algerian War of Independence was a bloody conflict, in which hundreds of thousands of people—many of them Algerian citizens—were killed.

determined to throw off the yoke of French control. Among the most strident of these groups was the Movement for the Triumph of Democratic Liberties (MTLD). When French authorities in Algeria suppressed the movement by rigging elections to favor the French settlers at the expense of Muslim Algerians, the MTLD formed a secret terrorist sub-organization, the Organisation Speciale (OS). By the time the Algerian insurrection began in earnest in the early 1950s, Ahmed Ben Bella had become the leader of the OS. He soon helped reorganize the OS as the Comité Révolutionnaire d'Unité et d'Action (Revolutionary Committee of Unity and Action, or CRUA). From Cairo, Egypt, Ben Bella and eight other Algerians—Hocine Ait Ahmed, Mohamed Boudiaf, Belkacem Krim, Rabah Bitat, Larbi Ben M'Hidi, Mourad Didouche, Moustafa Ben Boulaid, and Mohamed Khider—began preparing to fight for their independence. By October 1954, CRUA had renamed itself *Front de Libération Nationale* (National Liberation Front, or FLN).

Although the unrest over Algeria's status had been brewing for some time, the real fight for Algerian independence began on November 1, 1954. FLN guerrillas attacked a number of French targets inside Algeria, including military bases, police stations, and government buildings. FLN leaders broadcast messages from Cairo to Algerian Muslims, urging them to join the fight for "restoration of the Algerian state—sovereign, democratic, and social—within the framework of the principles of Islam." The French response was immediate—it would fight to keep Algeria as part of the French Republic.

Over the next eight years, and at the cost of perhaps as many as one million lives, Algerians fought for independence against the French, who became ever more ruthless in their quest to maintain control over the colony. But for all the talk of independence and nationalism, the men who started the movement for Algerian independence were more interested in taking control of the country for themselves than achieving freedom for their fellow citizens. Edgar O'Ballance, in his study *The Algerian Insurrection: 1954–1962*, wrote:

> Far from being a simple national movement springing from the mass of the people to throw off the French colonial yoke, it was begun by a small group of power-hungry men, shrewd, ambitious, and ruthless, who had little in common with the half-starved Algerian peasant. . . . The ideal . . . was that of nationalism, but this had to be discovered, polished up and then forced upon the people, who knew nothing of it.

By 1961, after almost a decade of violence, it was clear that General Charles de Gaulle, who had become the president of France, was willing to grant Algerian independence. This was an intolerable situation for the millions of French settlers living in Algeria. The settlers formed a terrorist organization known as the Organisation de l'Armee Secrete (Secret Army Organization, or OAS) to try to turn the tide. Despite a brutal campaign of terrorism, intimidation, and torture—in March 1962 the OAS set off an average of 120 bombs per day, many targeting schools and hospitals—the OAS failed. A referendum election on the question of Algerian independence was held in July 1962. The results were overwhelming: six million people out of a total electorate of 6.5 million cast their ballots in favor of Algerian independence. On July 3, de Gaulle pronounced Algeria independent. (However, the new Algerian government proclaimed July 5—the 132nd anniversary of the French arrival in Algeria—as the official day of independence.)

French and Algerian sources disagree on the number of casualties during the eight-year revolution. Official French estimates are that 350,000 Algerians were killed, while the Algerian government estimates 1.5 million were killed and 2 million Algerian Muslims became refugees. The true figure is probably somewhere between these estimates.

INDEPENDENCE AND AFTERWARD

On September 25, 1962, the new National Assembly of the Democratic and Popular Republic of Algeria met for the first time. By the end of the next day, Ahmed Ben Bella had been elected premier, although he shared power with leaders from the military (represented by Colonel Houari Boumedienne) and other political factions. Ben Bella and the FLN promised his people a "revolutionary Arab-Islamic state based on the principles of socialism and collective leadership at home and anti-imperialism abroad."

But the new government of Algeria had plenty of problems to deal with. French managers had gone home, leaving factories and other businesses without anyone who knew how to run them. Unemployment topped out at a whopping 70 percent. Public services were nonexistent for the same reason—the people who knew

Ahmed Ben Bella became the first premier of Algeria in September 1962, and was elected president the next year. However, his socialist regime was overturned just two years later, and he was arrested by the new president, Houari Boumedienne. Ben Bella remained in prison until 1980, when he was pardoned; he then spent 10 years in exile in Switzerland. Although Ben Bella returned to Algeria in 1990, and stood for election as a presidential candidate, he had little influence, and he retired from political life two years later.

Houari Boumedienne (1928–1978) became president of Algeria in 1965 and served until his death. During his regime a new Algerian constitution was written in 1976.

how to keep them running had long since departed for France. The Ben Bella regime nationalized much of the country's industry and agriculture, calling their program "Algerian Socialism."

In other socialist countries, such as the Soviet Union, collectivization of agriculture and nationalization of industry did not result in what rulers promised—a better standard of living for all citizens. This has also turned out to be true in Algeria. As a result, since Algeria won its independence the people have become poorer in relation to the rest of the world—even though the country could be a major producer of foodstuffs and could make huge profits on its high levels of oil and natural gas. Many of Algeria's current problems are a result of the socialist programs instituted by Ben Bella and others in the 1960s and 1970s.

Ben Bella's government ended in June 1965. Ben Bella tried to grab more power in the Algerian government; on June 19, 1965,

Colonel Boumedienne led a coup that overthrew the government, and Ben Bella was arrested. Boumedienne called his new government a "historic rectification," or correction, of the principles behind the Algerian War of Independence.

Boumedienne was a realist who sought to put the Algerian economy back on track. But his rule was not terribly secure at first, as his power base was more narrow than Ben Bella's had been. Most of Boumedienne's allies were members of the military, leaving him alienated from other branches of government.

To consolidate power, one of the first things Boumedienne did was to suspend the constitution Algeria had adopted in 1963. Then he appointed a 26-member body called the Council of the Revolution, which was designed to bring members of the military and the FLN together. Along with Boumedienne's own cabinet, the Council of Ministers, these men governed Algeria until Boumedienne's death in 1978.

During Boumedienne's regime, his government continued to pursue socialist economic policies. As part of its agenda, the government broke up the huge state-owned farms—which had originally been seized from individual landholders—and distributed small parcels of land to individual farmers. In return, these farmers had to work together to grow their crops, using equipment from the government to meet targets set by the regime in Algiers. These "social collectives" did not work as well as Algeria's rulers expected, and agricultural production continued to fall well below its potential. In fact, the nation was unable to meet its food needs on its own. Considering that thousands of years earlier Algerian farmers had fed the entire Roman Empire, this was quite a setback.

In April 1976, Boumedienne's government released a document called the National Charter, which contained the principles on which a new Algerian constitution would be based. The constitution was publicly debated for several months, until the government declared it official in November 1976. In the first election under the new constitution, Boumedienne was elected president with 95 percent of the vote.

After Boumedienne's death on December 27, 1978, a power struggle within the ruling FLN party ensued for control of the nation. After several months of squabbling, a candidate acceptable to both sides, Colonel Chadli Bendjedid, was sworn in as the new president of Algeria on February 9, 1979.

One of the first things Bendjedid did was to implement a five-year economic plan for Algeria. To expand the economy he decided to break up the large state-owned corporations. However, these measures did not immediately improve the lives of many ordinary Algerians. By 1987, Bendjedid had decided to dismantle Algeria's socialist system, which had clearly failed.

However, the constant economic troubles had already led growing numbers of Algerians to turn to fundamentalist Islam. Many figured that if a government based on nonreligious values was not able to provide for the people, perhaps a government that was more deeply rooted in religion could be more effective. By 1982, demonstrators were calling for a new Algerian government based on Islamic principles. **Islamist** protests began to occur on a broader scale, particularly on college campuses. In October 1988—a month that would become known as Algeria's "Black October"—Islamic groups rioted in several cities, destroying FLN property in the process. These demonstrations were violently put down by security forces. During the riots 500 people were killed and another 3,500 arrested.

Many people were outraged about the brutal measures used to put down the Black October riots. In response to their protests, Bendjedid replaced many senior officials and implemented a new program of political reform. In February 1989, a new Algerian constitution was approved overwhelmingly. This constitution

Chadli Bendjedid was a compromise choice for president after the 1978 death of Boumedienne. After 13 difficult years, he was forced to resign in 1992.

guaranteed freedoms of expression and association; at the same time, in response to the concerns of traditional Islamists, it withdrew guarantees of female rights that had appeared in the 1976 constitution.

In local and provincial elections held in June 1990, FLN candidates were defeated by representatives of a new party, the ***Front Islamique du Salut*** (Islamic Salvation Front, or FIS). When Bendjedid's government tried to change the election laws to help the FLN, the FIS protested and called for a general strike. From July to September 1991, Algeria was under martial law. Bendjedid appointed his minister of foreign affairs, Sid Ahmed Ghozali, to form a government that would bring Algerians together; although the FIS supported this goal, it continued to protest. In December

Muslim men sit in the streets of Algiers during a 1990 demonstration organized by the Islamic Salvation Front (FIS). The FIS was a political party that represented Muslim fundamentalists; its goal was to overthrow the secular government of Algeria led by Bendjedid, and to replace it with a government based on Islamic law.

1991, the FIS won 188 seats in the national assembly, far ahead of the FLN's 15 seats. This was a stunning victory for the Islamist cause.

Bendjedid's cabinet, terrified that the victory would lead to an absolute takeover by the FIS, forced the president to resign in January 1992. In the midst of the chaos, a group of Algerian generals took over the country. The era of rule by the FLN in Algeria was over, as was the brief period of electoral reform under Bendjedid. What was just beginning, however, was an era of brutal civil war in which over 100,000 Algerians—most of them civilians— would lose their lives.

The FIS seemed likely to win more power in the 1992 elections, so the military government cancelled the elections. The new government also outlawed the FIS, which then split into moderate and extremist wings.

After the turmoil of 1992, a series of Algerian leaders came and went. The first was General Muhammad Boudiaf; he was assassinated in June 1992, and General Ali Kalfa took over the presidency. He was turned out in 1994 by another general, Liamine Zéroual, who was initially seen as a moderate who might help reunite Algeria. However, Zéroual soon began a policy of cracking down on Islamic fundamentalists. During his rule the constitution was amended in 1996. The changes banned political parties based on religion (particularly fundamentalist Islam) or language (such as Berber parties) and expanded the president's power; it also limited the president to two five-year terms in office and made Islam the official religion of Algeria. Zéroual stepped down in 1999 after Abdelaziz Bouteflika was elected president.

Throughout the 1990s, Islamic militants were active throughout the country, and terrorized the civilian population in an attempt to take control of Algeria. In many cases, entire villages would be slaughtered in one night, and for a time the military was powerless

Demonstrators run from police during riots April 26, 2001, in the Berber city of Tizi Ouzou, Kabylia, located 62 miles (100 km) east of Algiers. The Berbers have protested attempts to destroy their language and culture; in the fall of 2001 the Algerian government agreed to recognize Berber as an official language.

to stop them. One of the most notorious of these militant organizations was the Groupes Islamiques Armées (Armed Islamic Group, or GIA), which attacked Algerian journalists, intellectuals, politicians, and educators, as well as European visitors to the country. Members of Algeria's Berber minority were also targets for the Islamists, possibly because of the Berbers' moderate Islamic views.

The Islamist movement lost support among many Algerians because of the brutal tactics used to spread terror through the country. In September 1997, the FIS declared a truce, but a new wave of terrorism indicated that FIS leaders had no control over the many radical factions. In January 2000, the armed wing of the FIS, the Islamic Salvation Army, disbanded. Many militants surrendered under an amnesty program offered by President Bouteflika. However, fighting has not completely ended in the country, and Algeria's economic problems remain unsolved.

The Berber minority, however, has opposed both the Islamists and the government. During 2000 and 2001, Berber residents of the Kabylia region demonstrated against the imposition of Arab language and culture. In October 2001, the Algerian government agreed to officially recognize Berber language and other Berber demands for equal treatment.

An oil refinery in Hassi Messaoud. Oil is a key part of Algeria's economy; the sale of oil and petroleum products accounts for most of the country's export revenue.

Politics, Religion and the Economy

In April 1999, after almost a decade of violence in which more than 100,000 Algerians were killed, the people of Algeria prepared once again to go to the polls in the hope that a new leader could bring some stability to the nation. Although eight candidates were scheduled to be on the ballot, seven of them withdrew before a single vote was cast. They believed that the election had been rigged, and took themselves out of the race in protest. In the end, this ensured the victory of the only remaining candidate—the one whom everyone thought had been ordained to win well before election day.

That man was Abdelaziz Bouteflika. On April 27, 1999, he was inaugurated as president of Algeria for a five-year term. Bouteflika's goals were clear: bring peace to the country; crack down on the terrorist activities of Islamist guerrillas;

In April 1999 Abdelaziz Bouteflika was elected president of Algeria. Many Algerians felt the election was rigged, and voter participation was very low. Nonetheless, Bouteflika has succeeded in reducing much of the unrest that nearly tore the country apart during the 1990s.

and try to stabilize the economy, which would allow Algerians to get back to work and entice foreigners to invest money in Algerian businesses.

During his term Bouteflika has managed to accomplish some of these goals, and the terrible massacres that used to occur in Algeria during the 1990s are much more rare—although the violence has by no means been eliminated entirely.

Part of Bouteflika's success in curbing the activities of the Islamic rebels has resulted from his offer of amnesty to any guerrilla who did not commit "blood crimes," which encompassed rape or murder (both of which were specialties of the Islamist terrorists). As a result, many rebels—80 to 85 percent, according to some estimates—have received a second chance to reenter Algerian society under the "Civil Concord."

A committed group of Islamic guerrillas still operates in Algeria. These are people who have no interest in receiving the government's amnesty, not only because they want to topple the regime and install an Islamic government, but also because they would not qualify for amnesty because of their crimes. By 2002, the remaining Islamist rebels in Algeria were responsible for an estimated 100 to 120 deaths each month—a high number, but less than one-tenth the average monthly death total of the mid-1990s.

THE GOVERNMENT OF ALGERIA

Despite its turbulent post-independence history, Algeria today has a legislative system that—at least in theory—works to represent the will of the people.

In addition to the executive branch, which consists of the president (who is the head of state) and the prime minister (who oversees the operations of the government), Algeria also has a legislative branch and a judicial branch, much like the United States. And like the Congress of the United States, the legislative branch of Algeria is bicameral, meaning that it is divided into an upper and lower house.

The lower house of Algeria's legislature is the National People's Assembly. The 380 members of this body are supposed to be elected directly by the people for five-year terms. The upper house is known as the Council of Nations. This body consists of 144 members—one-third are appointed by the president and the rest are elected by a system of indirect voting. Members of the Council of Nations serve six-year terms, with elections for half of the members scheduled every three years.

In recent years parliamentary elections have been marred by violence, low turnout, and a general lack of confidence in the results. Before the May 2002 elections for the National People's Assembly, 25 people were killed in an attack by Muslim rebels just hours before polls were scheduled to open, and a total of 390 people are believed to have been killed in the weeks leading up to the election as fundamentalists sought to disrupt the voting. Berber militants, too, have done their part to show displeasure during national elections by stealing and burning ballot boxes in the Kabylia region.

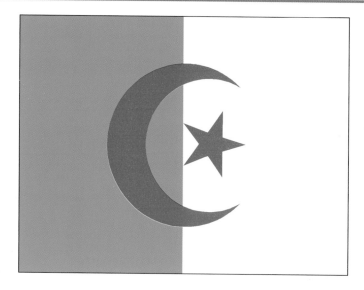

The Algerian flag was created in 1954, during the war for independence. It became the official flag of the newly independent state in July 1962. Green is the traditional color representing Islam, and the crescent and star are Islamic symbols as well; white is said to represent purity.

Algeria has a Supreme Court, which acts as the highest court in the land. The Supreme Court sits atop a judiciary system that includes *Daira* tribunals, which are the lowest courts and hear both civil and criminal cases, and *Wilaya* courts. *Wilaya* courts are located in each province, are run by three-judge panels, and have the authority to overrule the decisions of *Daira* tribunals on appeal.

ONE FAITH, MANY INTERPRETATIONS

Algeria is an almost entirely Muslim nation—citizens who do not accept the Qur'an as their holy book number in the thousands, out of a growing population of more than 30 million. Nearly all of the Muslims in Algeria are Sunni Muslims. (The Sunni are the largest group of Muslims worldwide; today, about 80 percent of the total Muslim population follows Sunni Islam.) Algeria is home to a small group of Ibadi Muslims, most of whom live in the M'zab Valley region. However, this group makes up less than half of 1 percent of the total Algerian population.

The central prayer and statement of belief for Muslims is a simple one: "There is no god but Allah, and Muhammad is his prophet." In fact, the word *Allah* literally translates as "the one God." This belief—called *shahada*—is one of the five most important beliefs of the Islamic faith. Other precepts, or pillars, of the religion include *salat*, the obligation that Muslims pray five times each day; *sawm*, the duty of fasting and observing certain rituals during the holy month of **Ramadan**; *zakat*, a compulsory tax that is paid to help the poor; and *hajj*, a requirement that all Muslims make a pilgrimage to Mecca, a city in modern-day Saudi Arabia that was the birthplace of Muhammad, at least once during their lifetime.

Muslims believe that their religion carries through all aspects of their lives. The Qur'an, which provides the teachings of Muhammad, and other writings are the basis for Islamic law, or *Sharia*. In a number of countries where Islam is the majority religion, *Sharia* is used as the basis for government laws. The individual behavior of every person in the country—whether they are Muslim or not—is governed by this law, which outlines everything from how a woman dresses to the types of food that can be consumed. In countries such as Iran, Saudi Arabia, and Sudan, *Sharia* is imposed in a harsh manner. The enforcement of *Sharia* was equally rigid in Afghanistan until the fall of the Taliban government in 2001. Islamists have been fighting for this type of government in Algeria.

However, since winning its independence Algeria has taken a more secular path in governing itself, and *Sharia* has never been implemented in any serious way. Although Islam is the country's official religion, the government of Algeria prohibits discrimination based on religion—in other words, those few Christians and Jews remaining in the country cannot be denied housing, jobs, and other necessities of life simply because they are not Muslims. Furthermore, unlike other Muslim countries, the Algerian government makes no inquiry into individuals' religious practices, considering them to be the private business of each person. Christian books, for example, are permitted in the country as long as they are for private use and not for missionary work. In many other Muslim countries, by contrast, Bibles are routinely taken away from travelers. However, the Algerian government does monitor the activities at certain mosques and of some preachers. This is done as a preventive measure—the government tries to watch for potential fundamentalist activities that could threaten the government or Algerian citizens.

One aspect of *Sharia* law that is applied in Algeria concerns the treatment of women. In 1984, in response to demands from fundamentalists, the government passed what is known as the Family Code. This set of laws instituted a variety of measures that discriminate against women. For example, under this code Algerian women are not legally considered adults no matter how old they are; instead, they are treated as minors, and their husband or another male relative acts as their official guardian. Algerian women are not permitted to marry without their father's consent; they cannot obtain a divorce except under very specific circumstances (although men may divorce their wives at any time); they are entitled to a smaller proportion of inheritances than their male relatives; and they do not always have full control over their own financial assets.

According to the U.S. State Department, which issues annual reports on religious freedom in countries around the world, the attitude of the Algerian government toward religion is similar to that of neighboring North African states like Morocco, Libya, and Tunisia. All of these countries, while proclaiming support for Islam to one degree or another, tend to take a fairly hands-off attitude towards the actual practice of the religion. Furthermore, all of the above-mentioned countries have small (generally less than 1 percent) minorities of Christians and Jews, and those communities are reportedly allowed to practice their religions without interference from the government or any religious authority.

This approach to Islam is far different from that advocated by Algeria's extremist Islamic fundamentalists. These people, represented by the FIS and other Islamist groups, wish to turn Algeria into a strict Muslim state. Considering the brutal tactics of their supporters, which at the height of the conflict regularly included the annihilation of entire villages, one can only imagine how such a regime might maintain control. In other countries where Islamic fundamentalists have taken over, such as Iran, women have virtually no rights (making Algeria's current treatment of women appear liberated by comparison); people are punished violently and publicly for violating Muslim teachings; and in some cases, radios, televisions, music, and even kite-flying have been banned. Although fundamentalists have used Algeria's economic problems as a springboard to denounce the current system and attract support for their own cause, most Algerian citizens recognize that the Islamist movement has caused far more problems than it has solved.

THE ALGERIAN ECONOMY

Algeria's economy is largely dependent on oil. Even though the country has traditionally enjoyed a strong agricultural sector, today the sale of oil and related products account for more than 95 percent of the country's foreign income. Oil also provides the country's government with 60 percent of the money it requires to operate, and contributes 30 percent of the country's overall ***gross domestic product (GDP)***, a measure of the total value of goods and services produced in the country each year. Algeria ranks among the world's most petroleum-rich nations: the country has the planet's fifth-largest reserves of natural gas and the fourteenth-largest reserves of crude oil.

Along with petroleum, Algeria's economy also relies on farming and industry, although the end products of these activities tend to be consumed entirely within the country. For example, Algeria manages to produce about 70 percent of the agricultural products it consumes in a year, but sells very little overseas. In recent years, however, the amount of Algerian land being farmed has increased, and many people are optimistic that agriculture will one day grow to the point where the country can export more of its crops. An increase in exports will diversify the economy and provide additional income to supplement the money Algeria makes from oil.

Despite Algeria's resources of potential wealth, it remains a

poor nation. Its current struggles are in part the result of the failed socialist policies of the 1960s and 1970s, as well as the upheaval during the Islamic insurgency of the 1990s, bad economic planning by the government, and official corruption. The weakness of Algeria's economy can be seen in a comparison of the GDP per capita of Algeria (about $1,630 in 2001, according to figures from the World Bank, which ranked the country 114th in the world) with that of the United States ($34,870,

An Algerian farmer walks between rows of young plants in Aoulef ech Cheurfa. Agriculture is an important part of Algeria's economy, and about 17 percent of the population is employed in farm-related jobs.

The Economy of Algeria

Gross domestic product (GDP*): $53.009 billion

GDP per capita: $1,630

Inflation: 3%

Natural resources: petroleum, natural gas, iron ore, phosphates, uranium, lead, zinc

Industry (33% of GDP): petroleum, natural gas, light industries, mining, electrical, petrochemical, food processing

Services (50% of GDP): government, other

Agriculture (17 % of GDP): wheat, barley, oats, grapes, olives, citrus, fruits, sheep, cattle

Foreign trade:

Imports—$1 billion—capital goods, food and beverages, consumer goods

Exports—$20 billion—petroleum, natural gas, and petroleum products

Currency exchange rate: 77.14 Algerian dinars = U.S. $1 (October 2002)

*GDP, or gross domestic product, is the total value of goods and services produced in a country annually. All figures 2001 estimates unless otherwise indicated. Sources: CIA World Factbook, 2002; World Bank

7th in the world on the World Bank's 2001 ranking); with France, Algeria's former colonial master ($22,690, ranked 24th); or with that of another oil-rich country, Kuwait ($18,030, ranked 31st). Furthermore, Algeria's unemployment rate currently hovers around 30 percent, although that figure is an improvement from the whopping rate of 50 percent during the mid-1990s.

In some respects the Algerian situation has been improving: rising oil prices in the year 2000 helped give the economy a much-needed boost in revenue. In addition, some of Algeria's foreign debt—the money it owes to other countries—has been forgiven. As a result, more money has stayed in the country to stimulate the economy.

The flames at the oil refinery in the background indicate gas burn-off; in the foreground are pipes that carry oil to Algerian ports. This refinery at Hassi Messaoud was built in 1997 by the Japan Gas Corporation. In recent years, the Algerian government has been more open to foreign investment, in hopes this would stimulate the country's economy.

However, these positive trends have not been enough to pull Algeria out of its financial difficulties. The Islamic insurgency created a ripple effect throughout the economy: valuable resources had to be diverted to the military to put down the rebels, and the unrest allowed official corruption to flourish. Furthermore, a large "underground" economy exists in Algeria, and these revenues are not reported to the government.

A major part of the Algerian economy's problems has been its history of socialist economics. Under a socialist economic system, the government controls most of the vital resources of the country—especially, in Algeria's case, vast oilfields—and businesses and individuals pay high taxes so that the state can provide a variety of services to the people. However, the downside is that it becomes more difficult to start new businesses or attract foreign investments, which make it hard for the economy to grow. History has shown that these types of socialist programs have failed everywhere they have been tried, and around the world many socialist nations have had to reduce the restrictions and controls that they have placed on their economies in an effort to encourage business development.

Under the Bouteflika administration, the government has turned over many formerly state-run companies to private ownership. In 2000, the government issued new rules making investment in the country more attractive to foreigners.

Today, many observers believe that under the right circumstances Algeria's economy has the potential to grow far beyond its current state. In fact some feel this is already happening. In 2000, the nation's GDP grew by 5 percent, and in 2001 it expanded by 4 percent. These encouraging signs indicate that economic reforms and political stabilization measures have started to take root.

But sustaining this growth will not be easy. Although Bouteflika's reforms have gone part of the way towards increasing the power of the economy, they have not gone far enough. With the exception of the oil industry, investment from companies outside Algeria is relatively rare. Without foreign investment, industries outside the petroleum sector will have trouble growing to the point where they can sell their products overseas, and the economy will continue to depend to a great degree on oil and natural gas.

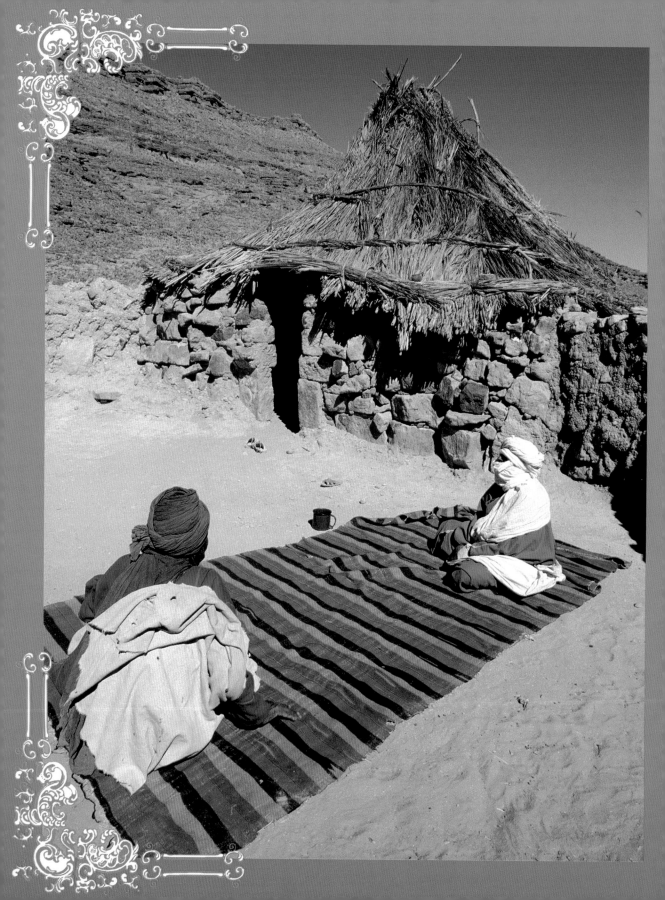

Tuareg tribesmen, wearing turbans and scarves to protect their faces, sit on a woven rug outside their hut. The Tuareg are a nomadic people who live in southern Algeria, and make up a very small percentage of the country's population. Most Algerians are ethnic Arabs, while the Berbers comprise the second-largest segment of the country's 32 million people.

The People

To be an Algerian means one is an heir to thousands of years of civilization while at the same time a citizen of a young nation.

Algeria's more than 32 million people are not a uniform lot. One can use statistics to paint a general picture of the population, however. Over 99 percent of the population is Muslim. Until the early 1960s there was a moderately sized Jewish population; however, most Jews fled the country when it became clear that those who did not follow Islam would not receive status as citizens of the new state. Today, the U.S. Department of State estimates that Algeria has a tiny Christian population (around 25,000 people, most of them Roman Catholics), and an even smaller Jewish community of perhaps fewer than 100 people.

Most Algerians are ethnically Arab—that is, they are the descendants of the warriors from the Arabian Peninsula who spread Islam, sword in hand, more than a thousand years ago. Those Algerians who trace their ancestry back to the Arabian Peninsula identify with a broader ethnic group beyond their fellow citizens. However, approximately 30 percent of Algeria's population are members of Berber tribes who lived in the region thousands of years before the arrival of the Arabs.

For a long time, these Berbers have felt as if they were second-class citizens in a country that was ruled by Arabs. This feeling dates all the way back to the original arrival of the Arabs. Even then, there were tensions between the two groups. Despite the Berbers long-standing presence in Algeria, and the fact that they not only resisted the invasion of French forces in the 19th century but helped drive out the Europeans in the 20th century, Berbers in the southern and central parts of the country have been discriminated against in the years since independence. In response, Algeria's Berbers, especially those living in the Kabylia region, have risen up to protest their treatment.

To complicate matters more, intermarriage between the two groups has further blurred the line between who is an ethnic Arab and who is a Berber.

FAMILY LIFE IN ALGERIA

Algerian family life has traditionally been centered around the home, with men as the head of the family and the women, for the most part, as only second-class figures. This family dynamic was reinforced in 1984 with the passage of laws that gave force to old prejudices and stripped women of many of the rights of full citizens. As a result, a woman needs permission from her father to get married, and once she has taken a husband, that man becomes her legal guardian—no matter how old she is. This is a reflection of the Arab Muslim culture that has existed in Algeria for over a thousand years, and which believes that women are inferior to men. Still, these

Like the other countries of North Africa, most of Algeria's population is clustered along the Mediterranean coastline. Even though the fertile coastal area makes up only 15 percent of Algeria's total land area, it is home to 90 percent of the population. The Kabylia region, where many of Algeria's Berbers live, is located on the coast east of Algiers.

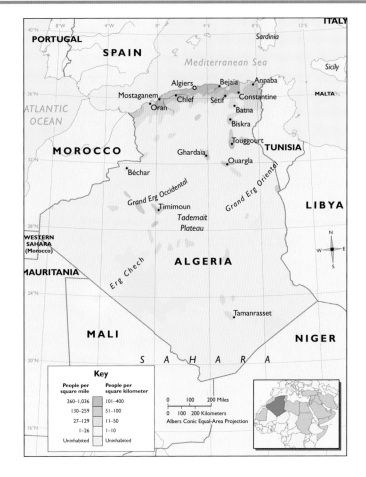

feelings are not uniform throughout Algeria, and attitudes towards women—and family in general—tend to be a lot more strict and conservative in villages and other rural areas than in the cities.

Along with the role of Algerian women, perhaps the most striking thing for a Westerner first encountering the Algerian family is its closeness. Extended families tend to live under one roof, especially in rural areas. Many generations can coexist together in giant compounds. In these settings, the entire family is responsible for raising children, even if couples live and eat separately from the family. This setup is not as common in the cities, and in recent years it has become more and more common for married couples to live together in their own house or apartment after their wedding.

Algerian children play with a soccer ball near Tindouf.

Weddings are another feature of family life that is far different in Algeria than in the West. Traditionally, marriages often were arranged—families matched the bride and groom on the basis of practical concerns rather than their child's love for his or her future spouse. However, arranged marriages have become less common. Algerian weddings also differ from Western weddings in their length—instead of just taking one afternoon or evening, Algerian wedding celebrations can last for several days, especially if the families involved are wealthy. And unlike in the West, where men and women celebrate together, in Algeria male and female wedding guests are traditionally given separate areas in which to eat and dance. Once married, a woman is expected to stay home to raise her children, and her status increases in the family and society if she bears sons.

Algerians value children, although boys are typically more highly prized than girls. (When an Arab man is asked how many children he has, it is not unusual for him to answer with the number of just his sons rather than with the total number of his children.) Boys and girls are raised together, although boys tend to get special treatment. The upbringing of girls, meanwhile, tends to concentrate on giving them the skills they will need to take care of their family in their adult life, including cooking, cleaning, and child care.

EDUCATION IN ALGERIA

With a growing population full of young people—more than one-third of the entire nation is under age 14—Algeria is deeply concerned about its education system, which not only must train its citizens to be productive but also provide them with a peaceful and stable nation in which their talents can be employed.

Today, all Algerian children must enter primary school (*ecole fondamentale*) at age 6. All students are supposed to remain in primary school until they reach 15 years of age, at which point they are supposed to continue on for three more years of high school (*ecole secondaire*). However, many students never receive this much education—in some cases, because they live too far away from a school to make it convenient for them to attend regularly, in other cases, because they have to drop out to help support their family. This has been especially true for girls, whose education has traditionally not been held to be as valuable as that of boys in Algeria. In recent years the United Nations and other organizations have developed projects to reverse the trend by integrating

The first word an Algerian infant hears is "Allah," as this is whispered into its ear almost immediately after birth.

female learning and literacy with income-generating activity for people in remote areas. However, Algeria's overall literacy rate—the percentage of the population over age 15 that can read and write—is fairly low at less than 62 percent.

While in primary school, students study a variety of subjects so they can make their way in the world. But because the Algerians have tried to "Arabize" as much of their social system as possible, many Algerian children who go to public school learn only Arabic. This is a problem, since French remains an important language of business in Algeria, and two of the country's three most important newspapers are printed in French.

After finishing *ecole fondamentale*, an Algerian child may go on to a general, specialized, or technical secondary school, depending on what they want to study and what sort of career they would like to have. After *ecole secondaire*, Algerians have the option of continuing their education, either at one of the universities administered by the Ministry of Education or at a more-advanced technical school.

ARTS AND CULTURE

Just as with most areas of Algerian life, Islam has a great influence on the arts and culture of the country. Traditionally, Muslims avoid making pictures or sculptures of living people or objects because the Qur'an prohibits it and considers it an affront to Allah. Instead, Algerians have incorporated ornate and difficult geometric patterns into their artwork, from tile mosaics that decorate architecture to colorful carpets. Algerian mosques are among the best places to see beautiful examples of creative Algerian pattern work, as well as the elaborate carpet and textile crafts that have been popular for centuries.

The Algerian carpet-making industry has been traditionally centered in the town of Ghardaia, in the M'Zab Valley. Like nearly all carpets of the Arab world, Algerian carpets are highly prized both for their quality of workmanship and their elaborately patterned designs. Although the country's recent troubles have kept tourists from making their way into the country to pick up examples of the art for their homes, it used to be possible to purchase rugs for very reasonable prices.

Carpets have been a part of Algerian culture for centuries—a legacy that has perhaps contributed to such myths as the famous "flying carpet." Before they were prized as works of decorative art around the world, they were everyday objects used for a variety of purposes. Perhaps most famously, carpets have been used as prayer rugs. In mosques, although there is no religious requirement for their presence, carpets have been used to make worshippers

A decorative example of Berber carpet. Weavers often use intricate designs and geometric patterns in their carpets because of Islamic rules against depicting people.

(who must take off their shoes before entering the building) more comfortable and to keep their feet and knees from getting cold as they bow and pray. And Muslim travelers have long carried so-called "prayer rugs" (traditionally, small rugs with a pattern that points at one end) to place on the ground facing in the direction of the holy city of Mecca before doing their daily prayer routine.

Pottery and ceramics are another tradition that has a long and storied history in Algeria. In fact, archaeologists have found pieces of Roman pottery in Algeria dating back 2,500 years—long before the Arab invasion.

While carpets and ceramics are ancient Algerian traditions that have changed little—with the possible exception of the final uses of the product—music is a field in which Algerians have made a mark in modern times. A form of music called "new Rai" or "modern Rai" has been popular since the 1960s, and is known for its driving, danceable rhythms. ("Rai" rhymes with "eye" and is untranslatable, except to say that it reflects a certain hip, cool attitude.) Much like rock music when it first debuted in the United States, Rai music has been very controversial, with many conservative Muslim leaders denounced the style as being un-Islamic,

The People of Algeria

Population: 32,277,942

Ethnic groups: Arab 74%, Berber 25%, European less than 1%

Religions: Sunni Muslim (state religion) more than 99%; Ibadi Muslim, Christian, Jewish, other, less than 1%

Age structure:
0–14 years: 33.5%
15–64 years: 62.4%
65 years and over: 4.1%

Population growth rate: 1.68%

Birth rate: 22.34 births/1,000 population

Death rate: 5.15 deaths/1,000 population

Infant mortality rate: 39.15 deaths / 1,000 live births

Life expectancy at birth:
total population: 70.24 years
males: 68.87 years
females: 71.67 years

Total fertility rate: 2.63 children born/woman

Literacy: 61.6% (1995 est.)

All figures are 2002 estimates unless otherwise indicated.
Source: CIA World Factbook, 2002

immoral, and corrupting. Most offensive to these clerics was the fact that women were able to succeed at becoming popular singers of the genre, and that many of the Rai song lyrics dealt with romantic love. The low point of the controversy came in 1994, when the Rai singing star Cheb Hasni was shot and killed by Islamic radicals in Oran.

The Berber tribes in southern and central Algeria have their own unique arts and crafts that have contributed to the country's creative heritage. These nomadic, wandering tribes are not only famous within the country for their patterned metal and woodwork; their influences on Algerian artists of Arab descent are also evident. Primarily because of their need to be able to carry everything they owned from place to place as they wandered the desert, Berbers have traditionally channeled much of their creative energy into making objects like silver bracelets, pendants, earrings, swords, and daggers. Berber designs have been embraced and integrated into the work of Algerian artists of all ethnic backgrounds.

Plowed fields and orchards are next to blocks of apartment
buildings in this photograph of the outskirts of Tlemcen. This city
on Algeria's northwestern coast is said to have the most beautiful
mosques in North Africa.

Communities

Algeria is a beautiful country, with a variety of interesting natural features and old cities that are attractive to tourists. However, in recent years the violence in the country has limited opportunities for foreigners to visit Algeria's many vibrant communities.

ALGIERS

With a population of 1,650,300, Algeria's capital city is also its largest city. And given that there has been some sort of settlement in the area since Phoenician times, it is also one of Algeria's oldest settlements. Although much of the city's precolonial architecture was destroyed by the French naval bombardment and subsequent invasion in 1830, there is still an old district of the city where one can see ancient Arab architecture. On these tight, narrow streets one can get a sense of how Algerians would have lived before the arrival of the French, and also of the poverty that has descended on the nation in recent decades.

The loss of this architectural heritage was something that even Alexandre Dumas, with all his pride in France and French achievement, regretted in his report on Algeria. "The buildings begin at the water's edge and climb the whole eastern slope of the mountain," Dumas wrote in 1846 after seeing the city for the first time. "French buildings have completely spoiled the Eastern atmosphere that formerly characterized Algiers, so that now, at first sight, it looks almost European."

Today, while most travelers would find the French architecture of the 19th century charming and not regret for a moment the transformation, the addition of many slums—the result of decades of poverty in the 20th century—has diminished the charm of this ancient port.

Algiers is the center of much of Algeria's commercial and government life, and many of the people who live in the city work for either the government or one of its agencies or corporations. And partially due to France's long involvement in the city—most of the French who settled in Algeria during colonial times lived in Algiers—there is a strong tradition of museums and other cultural institutions which are surprisingly vital and do their best to preserve the nation's heritage. Among the best is the Museum of Popular Arts and Tradition. Housed in a spectacular palace that was built by the Ottomans and later became the Algiers Town Hall, today the museum holds an excellent collection of rugs, jewelry, native costumes, and pottery.

Oran

Located on the Algerian coast to the west of Algiers, Oran is the second-largest city in the country with a population of approximately 712,300.

The sun sets over Algiers, the capital of Algeria. Centrally located on the Mediterranean coast, Algiers is the most important city in the country.

Unlike Algiers, with its ancient history, Oran is relatively new. It was founded by Arab sailors in the 10th century as a trading post. In later years, it was occupied by a series of powers, including the Spanish and the Turks, until the French finally seized control in 1831 as part of their drive to conquer Algeria. Today the city is still a major port for Algeria, with passenger and cargo ships from Europe arriving and departing regularly.

The French novelist Albert Camus (1913–1960) was born in Oran, and used the city as the setting for two of his most famous works, *L'Etranger* (*The Stranger*, 1942) and *La Peste* (*The Plague*, 1947). Camus received the Nobel Prize for Literature in 1957. Another famous person who was born in Oran is the French fashion designer Yves Saint Laurent.

CONSTANTINE

As the name suggests, Constantine is an ancient city, dating back even before the days of the Byzantine emperor who gave the town its current name. It is Algeria's oldest continuously inhabited settlement. More than half a million people live in Constantine, which is east of Algiers and just inland from the coast.

The most dramatic thing about Constantine is its location. It is perched high up in the mountains, and cliffs descend from the main section of the city into deep valleys and gorges. This is quite a dramatic setting, especially with the presence of the four great bridges that cross the main gorge known as the Rhumel. (Sadly, in recent years, the natural beauty of the setting has been tarnished by the fact that the deep crevasses around the city have served as garbage dumps.)

Because of its easily defended, hard-to-attack location, Constantine has been a military outpost for thousands of years; any empire that was lucky enough to capture it was sure to hold the area for quite some time. To illustrate the difficulty of taking

Constantine is the oldest continuously-inhabited settlement in Algeria.

Constantine, one need look no further than the fact that it took until 1937 for the French, with all their modern military technology, to finally bring the city under their control.

THE KABYLIA REGION

The Kabylia region, one of the most scenic in Algeria, is notable for its high concentration of Berbers. The Berbers of Kabylia have a strong cultural identity, and nearly all prefer to use their own language rather than Arabic or French. In 2001, after protests throughout Kabylia, the government of Algeria finally declared Berber language to be an official language of Algeria.

Members of Berber tribes live together in villages throughout the region. A form of Berber music that originated in this area, Kabyle, is played with traditional instruments such as the *bendir* (frame drum), *t'bel* (tambourine), *ajouag* (flute), and *ghaita* (a type of bagpipe). A Berber singer named Matoub Lounès combined Kabyle with Rai, another form of Algerian music, and gained great popularity during the 1990s. Many of his songs protested the civil war and repression of Berber culture. After he was killed by Islamists in the Atlas Mountains in 1998, he became a martyr for the Berber cause.

Kabylia is the greenest part of Algeria, with a dramatic landscape that appeals to travelers. Winters can be harsh and long in the region, though spring and summer are more moderate.

RELIGIOUS CELEBRATIONS

The most important celebrations in the Algerian calendar focus on the Islamic holidays. However, because the Muslim calendar is based on the cycles of the moon and not the Western 365-day calendar, one cannot easily predict the exact dates of these events from year to year. The most significant religious observances for Muslims everywhere—not just in Algeria—are Ramadan, Eid al-Fitr,

> According to the Qur'an, during Ramadan the day's fasting begins as soon as one can distinguish a black thread from a white thread in daylight.

and Eid al-Adha.

During Ramadan, Muslims are supposed to fast from sunrise to sunset. This means that they are not supposed to eat anything, drink anything (not even water), or smoke anything during those hours of the day, in the belief that one's spirit will be purified as a result of denying the body material and worldly pleasure. And along with denying themselves food and drink, Muslims must also act in a spiritual manner—all the good a person does in a day's fasting can be undone by lying, speaking poorly about another behind his or her back, or acting in a jealous or covetous manner.

Because the Islamic calendar is based on the cycle of the moon, Ramadan takes place at a different time every year. In fact, it is hard to say with exact certainty when it will begin and end in any given year. While many religions have some form of ritual annual fasting and self-denial—such as Yom Kippur in Judaism or Lent in traditional sects of Christianity—this is one of the most extreme periods of self-denial of any major faith. People in Algeria take Ramadan seriously, and streets are typically much less crowded during this period as people stay inside to work, rest, or contemplate the Qur'an until the evening, when they sit down to huge meals with their families.

If Ramadan is an occasion for self-denial, Eid al-Fitr is an occasion for celebration. This is perhaps the most important festival in the Islamic and Algerian calendar, as it represents the breaking of the fast of Ramadan. Lasting three days, Eid al-Fitr is a time when families get together in a spirit that could almost be compared to that of Christmas in the West. It is considered obligatory for Muslims to give a gift to the poor during this time, and children are

An Algerian family prepares a sheep for Eid al-Adha. This Islamic festival remembers the willingness of the patriarch Abraham to sacrifice his son to Allah; it also marks the end of the annual *hajj* period of pilgrimage to Mecca.

traditionally also given presents and new clothes. Eid al-Fitr is perhaps the most joyous festival of the Muslim calendar.

The other great festival of the Islamic calendar, Eid al-Adha, is literally translated as the "Festival of the Sacrifice." Eid al-Adha commemorates the willingness of the Old Testament patriarch Abraham to sacrifice his son to Allah. The festival goes on for four days and takes place approximately three months after Eid al-Fitr. It also marks the last day of the *hajj* season of pilgrimage, when millions of Muslims travel to Mecca to fulfill their religious duty.

Along with the important holy dates of Islam, the Algerian calendar has a number of celebrations connected with the country's history. Perhaps the two most important of these dates are July 5, Algeria's Independence Day, and November 1, which marks the beginning of the Algerian Revolution. Celebrations on these dates typically involve a great deal of patriotic speechmaking by officials and recollections of the revolutionary struggle against France, although the celebrations have also been used as excuses for violence or troublemaking by political groups representing the opposition.

Palestinian leader Yasir Arafat poses with a young Algerian girl during a 1988 visit to Algiers. Historically Algeria has supported the Palestinians in their quest for statehood. In recent years the country's leaders have called for a peaceful solution to the Israeli-Palestinian violence.

Foreign Relations

*I*n the four decades since it achieved independence, Algeria's relations with Europe and the United States have gradually become friendlier. In recent years, following the experiments with socialism and the nationalization of industry that marked the years after independence in 1962, the government in Algiers has committed itself to a program of economic liberalization. These plans for reform have occurred despite—or perhaps because of—the bloody conflict between the Algerian government and the Islamic fundamentalist rebels. The Algerian government aims to give its people a more comfortable economic life with lower rates of unemployment. By doing so, it hopes that there will be a clearer alternative for Algerians—especially the young and out of work—to the stark religious program of the insurgents.

Of course, while increasing economic freedoms and ties

with Western nations is a matter of economic and political survival, it is also a difficult agenda for an Arab country to undertake. The conflict between Israel and the Palestinians, as well as the U.S.-led war on terrorism, have many in the Arab world believing that Islamic Middle Eastern nations must stick together against the perceived threat from non-Muslim countries. Consequently, there is a great deal of pressure on those Arab leaders who wish for their nations to follow a different path.

ALGERIA AND EUROPE

Because 90 percent of Algeria's population lives along the Mediterranean, the country's obligation to maintain a relationship with Europe has always been clear. The country's closest ties are to France, its former colonial master. France took in nearly one million Algerian immigrants after Algeria won its independence in 1962; today, the Algerian community in France is the largest non-European ethnic group in Europe.

French-Algerian relations have changed many times in the decades since independence. Although at the time France and Algeria signed an agreement stating that France would provide military and medical assistance to the new country, in general the relationship was not close during Ben Bella's administration. After Boumedienne took over in 1965, he negotiated closer ties to France, and strengthened the Algerian army with French aid and training.

The relationship with France and the West was weakened when Algeria made a strategic alliance with the Soviet Union in the late 1960s. By the mid-1980s, however, the U.S.S.R. was having its own economic problems and could no longer supply financial aid to countries like Algeria. As a result, the Algerian government began to develop closer ties to the West.

When the military took over the government in 1992, and began to suppress the Islamist movement in Algeria, France provided some military aid to the Algerian government. In response Algerian rebels attacked French targets as well as Algerian ones. In 1994, terrorist members of the Armed Islamic Group hijacked an Air France jet in Algiers, holding the passengers hostage for several days. In 1995, a series of explosions in Paris killed 8 people and wounded 160. It is believed that some of the leaders of the Islamist movement worked with the large Algerian immigrant population in France to plan such activities. These attacks persuaded the French to back away from Algeria.

Since Bouteflika took over as president of Algeria in 1999, the ties have become closer again. Algeria imports more than $2 billion

French foreign minister Hubert Vedrine (right) greets his Algerian counterpart, Abdelaziz Belkhadem, at Algiers airport in 2001. Despite the ugliness of the Algerian War for Independence, today the two countries maintain a strong relationship.

each year in food and industrial equipment from France, and French oil companies continue to operate in the country.

Relations between Algeria and other countries in Europe have also been close. European nations purchase almost two-thirds of Algeria's exports and the government of Algeria has signed a number of agreements with the European Union. The most important of these are part of the series of agreements that began in 1979 to encourage economic cooperation between Algeria and the European continent. On December 19, 2001, the European Commission signed an "association agreement" with Algeria that had a series of goals in mind, both political and economic. Among them are the establishment of "regular political and economic dialogue," "strengthening economic co-operation," "setting up social and cultural co-operation," and the "gradual establishment of a free trade area."

Today, millions of people of Algerian descent live in Europe. Algerian emigration to Europe began during World War I, when Algerians joined the French army or moved to France to fill jobs vacated by French soldiers. After the war, an industrial boom created a need for unskilled laborers. Between 1920 and 1939, more than a million Algerians—many of them Arabs and Berbers—moved to France to find work, although some of them eventually returned to Algeria. After the Second World War, this immigration trend continued.

After Algeria won its independence, tens of thousands of the Algerians who were descended from the 19th-century French settlers left the country. Even greater numbers of Arab and Berber Muslims also left Algeria, though, and they and their descendants make up the largest part of the Algerian emigrant community today.

France has the largest population of Algerian immigrants, estimated at between 3 and 5 million people. Spain and Germany also have large populations of Algerian immigrants.

ALGERIA AND THE UNITED STATES

Algeria's relationship with the United States has changed over the years since the country won its independence from France in 1962. At that time it was the height of the Cold War between the United States and the Soviet Union, and the Algerian government under Ben Bella seemed to lean toward the side of the communists. Algeria instituted a socialist economic program, supported the communist Cuban dictator Fidel Castro, and during the 1960s backed other "anti-imperialist" movements for freedom from colonial control, particularly in Africa but also in such countries as Vietnam.

In many ways the close ties between the U.S. and France prevented closeness with Algeria, although the United States sent an ambassador to Algeria in 1962. After the June 1967 war between Israel (which was supported by the United States) and most of its Arab neighbors, Algeria broke diplomatic ties with the United States. The two countries remained estranged for more than a decade.

After Iranian militants attacked the American Embassy in Tehran, Iran, in 1979, taking 52 Americans hostage, the Algerian government helped negotiate the eventual safe release of the hostages. During the 1980s, trade and other avenues for diplomacy between the U.S. and Algeria developed as the relationship between Algeria and the Soviet Union weakened. By 1990, Algeria was importing more than $1 billion annually from the United States, and the U.S. was providing nearly $26 million in annual financial assistance.

When the Algerian military overthrew the government in 1992, the U.S. initially condemned the coup. However, it later seemed to accept the military government. The U.S. stance angered Islamist rebels, who accused the American government of neglecting the situation and allowing for the elimination of the democratic process

In July 2001, Abdelaziz Bouteflika became the first president of Algeria to visit the White House in 15 years. Since becoming president of Algeria in 1999, Bouteflika has worked to establish a closer relationship with the United States.

in Algeria. Throughout the civil war of the 1990s, the U.S. remained reluctant to get involved in the conflict.

In recent years, the administration of President Bouteflika has established even closer relations between the United States and Algeria. Algeria has worked with the United States to broker peace accords in places like Ethiopia, which in 2000 made peace with their neighbors the Eritreans, who clashed with Ethiopians in a prolonged border dispute. In 2001, Bouteflika became the first Algerian president to visit the White House in 15 years.

Economic ties between Algeria and the United States have been strengthened as well. In July 2001, the two nations signed a Trade and Investment Framework Agreement. In addition, through the U.S.–North African Economic Partnership (USNAEP), Algeria receives about $1.2 billion in aid from Washington each year. U.S. officials have expressed hope that such agreements will help the Algerian government privatize industries, which should lead to greater profits and efficiency for Algeria's economy. By strengthening the economy, both Algeria and the United States hope to encourage investors from overseas to buy and build businesses in

Algeria, giving more local citizens the opportunity to find and hold jobs.

Since terrorists attacked targets in the United States on September 11, 2001, Algeria has taken a firmly pro-American line, and supported the U.S.-led war on terrorism. Algeria's reaction is understandable, considering the terrorist threat that it had faced over the previous decade. As Algeria's ambassador to the United States, Idriss Jazairy, said in a speech to the Baltimore Council on Foreign Affairs in October 2001:

> Algerians are particularly sensitive to wanton murder, because they have been subject to the same violence. . . . Those who blaspheme God by doing evil in God's name, Islam is not their faith. Islam is a religion of faith, of moderation. We exercise tolerance and even-handedness. The terrorists are not Muslims.

ALGERIA AND THE ARAB WORLD

Since Algeria received its independence, its status as a member of the Arab community has never been in doubt. "The Algerians rightly claim kinship with the Arab world, in which they never feel they are foreigners," former ruler Ben Bella once said. "In Cairo, Baghdad, or Damascus, in spite of considerable differences, we always find something which suddenly reminds us that we are at home—the look of a street, a word, or a gesture, or some shared custom."

But this does not mean Algeria enjoys entirely happy relations with other Arab communities. As it turns out, some of the country's early efforts to help independence movements wound up rubbing would-be allies the wrong way. For example, in 1976 Algeria declared its support for the Polisario, a rebel group in Morocco that claimed the right of the southern section of that country to secede and become the independent nation of Western Sahara. Not surprisingly, the Moroccan government has taken a dim view of the

During the mid-1970s, Algeria supported a movement for independence in the region known as the Western Sahara. This sparsely populated desert territory, which borders the Atlantic Ocean between Mauritania and Morocco, is rich in phosphates and has productive offshore fishing grounds. It had been controlled by Spain until 1976, when it came under Moroccan control. However, members of a group called the Polisario (Frente Popular para la Liberación de Saguia el Hamra y Rio de Oro) demanded independence. Fighting between Morocco and the Polisario continued until 1991, when a United Nations cease-fire went into effect. A referendum vote to determine the status of the Western Sahara territory was scheduled for 1992; the vote has been put off several times, most recently in 2002. In the meantime, some members of the Polisario—including the women pictured waving Polisario flags above—have fled the Western Sahara and are living in refugee camps in Algeria.

Polisario's actions. Despite the difference of opinion, though, the two countries have worked to further restore friendly relations.

Algeria's relations with the rest of its neighbors are less stormy. In fact, the country is on good terms with the rest of its geographic

CHRONOLOGY

1830: French invade Algeria and sack Algiers in an effort to shore up popularity for King Charles X; though Charles is deposed soon after, the new government holds onto Algeria as a matter of national honor.

1834: France officially annexes Algeria.

1847: Western Algeria comes under French control.

1871: The French bring the Kabylie Mountain region into their area of control, establishing the borders of modern-day Algeria.

1935: Collective of religious leaders known as the *ulema* begin to make demands for Algerian independence.

1954: Algerian Insurrection officially begins November 1 after an uprising in the town of Batna.

1962: After eight years of conflict, France decides to pull out of Algeria after a national referendum indicates overwhelming support for independence; on September 25, the first Algerian legislature convenes, and Ahmed Ben Bella is named first premier of the new nation.

1963: The first Algerian constitution is written; Ben Bella is elected president.

1965: Colonel Houari Boumedienne leads coup on June 19, seizes power, and promises economic reform.

1978: Boumedienne dies, and a struggle for the leadership of Algeria ensues.

1979: Colonel Chadli Bendjedid is sworn in as president on February 9.

1982: Demonstrations by Islamic fundamentalists begin to occur around the country.

1988: "Black October" occurs; fundamentalists riot and destroy FLN property; in the ensuing crackdown, 500 people are killed and 3,500 arrested.

1989: FIS, or Islamic Salvation Front, is founded, despite ban on religiously oriented political parties.

1991: FIS sweeps elections, the results of which are invalidated by the government; Bendjedid is forced out by his cabinet, which seeks to restore control; Muhammad Boudiaf takes the reins of power.

1992: Boudiaf is assassinated in June; Ali Kalfa becomes president.

1994: Kalfa is turned out of government; General Liamine Zéroual becomes new leader of Algeria and begins a crackdown on Islamic fundamentalists.

1995: Zéroual wins widely boycotted presidential elections.

1999: Abdelaziz Bouteflika is elected president in April; Bouteflika takes new measures to combat the insurgency, including offering amnesty to rebels not involved in "blood crimes"—rape and murder.

2001: In response to Berber protests, the Algerian government agrees to recognize the Berber language as official.

2002: Legislative elections are held in the spring; FLN wins across the board after widespread boycotts and pre-election violence by fundamentalist forces.

2003: In February, an Arab League summit is held in Cairo, Egypt, to discuss the group's position on Iraq and its dictator, Saddam Hussein; in May, President Bouteflika replaces Ali Benflis with Ahmed Ouyahia as prime minister.

GLOSSARY

annex—to take over territory and incorporate it into another country.

Barbary Coast—a European term for the coast of North Africa, which comes from the name of the famous pirate Barbarossa.

Berbers—nomadic tribespeople of Algeria who have lived in the region for thousands of years.

Crusades—the name for a series of military expeditions, in the period 1095–1291, made by Christian Europeans to the Middle East in order to recapture areas held by Muslims.

dey—a term for rulers in Algeria who governed during the period between the decline of Ottoman influence and the French invasion (1671–1830).

Front Islamique du Salut (Islamic Salvation Front, or FIS)—political party, active during the 1990s, which represented Muslim fundamentalists who looked to overthrow the secular government of Algeria and replace it with *Sharia* law.

Front de Libération Nationale (National Liberation Front, or FLN)—an organization formed to fight for Algerian independence; it later became the ruling party in Algeria.

garrison—a body of troops stationed at a military post, or the post where troops are stationed.

gross domestic product (GDP)—a measure of the total value of goods and services produced in the country each year.

Ibadi Islam—a form of Islam that developed in the eighth century; it allows for the election of spiritual leaders called imams. Algeria has a small Ibadi population, which is primarily located in the M'zab Valley region.

imam—the leader of an Islamic community.

Islamist—espousing radically fundamentalist Islamic doctrine that is usually hostile to Western societies and ideas.

Janissaries—well-trained soldiers of the Ottoman Empire.

Maghreb—a name for the area of northwestern Africa that includes Algeria, Morocco, and Tunisia.

mercenary—a professional soldier paid to fight for an army other than that of his or her country.

monotheism—the belief that there is only one God.

GLOSSARY

oases—fertile areas in the desert where water is available and plants grow.

polytheistic—relating to a religion that worships more than one deity.

Qur'an—the Muslim holy book, which was dictated by the prophet Muhammad in the 7th century A.D.

Ramadan—the month of fasting observed by Muslims during which they abstain from food, drink, and tobacco from sunrise to sunset.

savanna—a flat grassland in a tropical or subtropical region.

Sharia—a civil legal code based on the Qur'an and other Islamic writings.

tribute—a payment made by one ruler or state to another as a sign of submission.

FURTHER READING

Connelly, Matthew James. *A Diplomatic Revolution: Algeria's Fight for Independence and the Origins of the Post–Cold War Era.* New York: Oxford University Press, 2002.

Crowther, Geoff, and Hugh Finlay. *Morocco, Algeria & Tunisia: A Travel Survival Kit.* Berkeley, Calif.: Lonely Planet Publications, 1989.

Dumas, Alexandre. *Adventures in Algeria.* Translated by Alma Elizabeth Murch. New York: Chilton Press, 1959.

Fanon, Frantz. *A Dying Colonialism.* Translated by Haakon Chevalier. New York: Grove/Atlantic, 1993.

————. *The Wretched of the Earth.* Translated by Constance Farrington. New York: Grove/Atlantic, 1976.

Grove, A.T. *The Changing Geography of Africa.* Oxford: Oxford University Press, 1994.

Joesten, Joachim. *The Red Hand.* London: Abelard-Schuman, 1962.

Laremont, Ricardo René. *Islam and the Politics of Resistance in Algeria, 1783–1992.* Trenton, N.J.: Africa World Press, 2000.

Merle, Robert. *Ben Bella.* London: Michael Joseph Press, 1965.

Messaoudi, Khalida. *Unbowed: An Algerian Woman Confronts Islamic Fundamentalism.* Translated by Anne C. Vila. Philadelphia: University of Pennsylvania Press, 1998.

O'Ballance, Edgar. *The Algerian Insurrection: 1954–1962.* Ithaca, N.Y.: Faber and Faber, 1967.

Quandt, William B. *Between Ballots and Bullets: Algeria's Transition from Authoritarianism.* Washington, D.C.: Brookings Institute Press, 1998.

Stevens, Valerie and Jon. *Algeria and the Sahara.* London: Constable, 1977.

Stora, Benjamin, and William B. Quandt. *Algeria, 1830–2000: A Short History.* Translated by Jane Marie Todd. Syracuse: Cornell University Press, 2001.

Willis, Michael. *The Islamist Challenge in Algeria.* New York: New York University Press, 1997.

http://www.hejleh.com/countries/algeria.html

A compilation of links to many special-interest Web sites focused on Algerian culture, politics, business, government, and history, among other topics.

http://www.algeria-interface.com

All the latest news and dispatches from Algeria.

http://i-cias.com/m.s/algeria/

A comprehensive Web page devoted to the cities and towns of Algeria.

http://www.algeria-un.org/

Official information from the Algerian foreign service.

http://www.cia.gov/cia/publications/factbook/geos/ag.html

The CIA World Factbook website provides a wealth of statistical information about Algeria.

http://memory.loc.gov/frd/cs/dztoc.html

This Library of Congress website is a detailed country study of Algeria, providing much historical information about the country before the early 1990s.

INDEX

Numbers in **bold italic** refer to captions.

INDEX

PICTURE CREDITS

CONTRIBUTORS

The **FOREIGN POLICY RESEARCH INSTITUTE (FPRI)** served as editorial consultants for the Modern Middle East Nations series. FPRI is one of the nation's oldest "think tanks." The Institute's Middle East Program focuses on Gulf security, monitors the Arab-Israeli peace process, and sponsors an annual conference for teachers on the Middle East, plus periodic briefings on key developments in the region.

Among the FPRI's trustees is a former Secretary of State and a former Secretary of the Navy (and among the FPRI's former trustees and interns, two current Undersecretaries of Defense), not to mention two university presidents emeritus, a foundation president, and several active or retired corporate CEOs.

The scholars of FPRI include a former aide to three U.S. Secretaries of State, a Pulitzer Prize–winning historian, a former president of Swarthmore College and a Bancroft Prize–winning historian, and two former staff members of the National Security Council. And the FPRI counts among its extended network of scholars—especially its Inter-University Study Groups—representatives of diverse disciplines, including political science, history, economics, law, management, religion, sociology, and psychology.

DR. HARVEY SICHERMAN is president and director of the Foreign Policy Research Institute in Philadelphia, Pennsylvania. He has extensive experience in writing, research, and analysis of U.S. foreign and national security policy, both in government and out. He served as Special Assistant to Secretary of State Alexander M. Haig Jr. and as a member of the Policy Planning Staff of Secretary of State James A. Baker III. Dr. Sicherman was also a consultant to Secretary of the Navy John F. Lehman Jr. (1982–1987) and Secretary of State George Shultz (1988).

A graduate of the University of Scranton (B.S., History, 1966), Dr. Sicherman earned his Ph.D. at the University of Pennsylvania (Political Science, 1971), where he received a Salvatori Fellowship. He is author or editor of numerous books and articles, including *America the Vulnerable: Our Military Problems and How to Fix Them* (FPRI, 2002) and *Palestinian Autonomy, Self-Government and Peace* (Westview Press, 1993). He edits *Peacefacts*, an FPRI bulletin that monitors the Arab-Israeli peace process.

From his first trip to Egypt as a high school student, **JAMES MORROW** has been fascinated by the Middle East. In the years since, he has had numerous opportunities to study and write about the region, first as a student at Georgetown University's School of Foreign Service and later as a journalist writing for a wide range of publications, including *U.S. News & World Report*, *National Review*, and *The Australian* newspaper. He currently divides his time between Sydney, Australia, and New York City, with his wife Claire (without whose research assistance this book would not have been possible) and their son, Nicholas.